Tell Me, Where Are We Going and How Do We Get There?

Ulf Lubienetzki • Heidrun Schüler-Lubienetzki

Tell Me, Where Are We Going and How Do We Get There?

What Matters When Facilitating Groups

Ulf Lubienetzki
entwicklung GbR
Hamburg, Germany

Heidrun Schüler-Lubienetzki
entwicklung GbR
Hamburg, Germany

ISBN 978-3-662-65587-0   ISBN 978-3-662-65588-7 (eBook)
https://doi.org/10.1007/978-3-662-65588-7

© Springer-Verlag GmbH Germany, part of Springer Nature 2022
The translation was done with the help of artificial intelligence (machine translation by the service DeepL.com). A subsequent human revision was done primarily in terms of content.
This work is subject to copyright. All rights are reserved by the Publisher, whether the whole or part of the material is concerned, specifically the rights of translation, reprinting, reuse of illustrations, recitation, broadcasting, reproduction on microfilms or in any other physical way, and transmission or information storage and retrieval, electronic adaptation, computer software, or by similar or dissimilar methodology now known or hereafter developed.
The use of general descriptive names, registered names, trademarks, service marks, etc. in this publication does not imply, even in the absence of a specific statement, that such names are exempt from the relevant protective laws and regulations and therefore free for general use.
The publisher, the authors and the editors are safe to assume that the advice and information in this book are believed to be true and accurate at the date of publication. Neither the publisher nor the authors or the editors give a warranty, expressed or implied, with respect to the material contained herein or for any errors or omissions that may have been made. The publisher remains neutral with regard to jurisdictional claims in published maps and institutional affiliations.

This Springer imprint is published by the registered company Springer-Verlag GmbH, DE, part of Springer Nature.
The registered company address is: Heidelberger Platz 3, 14197 Berlin, Germany

Preface

For more than two decades, we have been dealing professionally with human communication. Whether as coaches, trainers, consultants, or even as managers, it is always about exchanging factual information, communicating personal perceptions, and feelings, evaluating something or even someone, or achieving something together with one or more people. In the course of time, we have gathered a lot of our own experience in communication and have developed our knowledge in a targeted manner. An important part of our work is passing on our experience and knowledge to our clients. In our profession, this is mostly done in the form of seminars, trainings, and workshops. The great advantage of seminars, trainings, and workshops, be it in the presence or online variant, is that it is possible to specifically address the individual questions and needs of the participants. Therefore, the most important component of our events is always working on participant's case studies and developing solutions together. Then we proceed with challenging these solutions in our discussion with the group. Inevitably, the possibilities of reaching people with seminars on communication topics are limited. The cooperation with various universities as well as with Springer Verlag offers us the opportunity to reach significantly more people. We were and are aware that it is in the nature of publications not to be able to respond directly to individual questions and examples from readers. We have, therefore, seen it as our essential task to convey the knowledge we have compiled on various communication topics as clearly and as closely as possible to what is possible in seminars and training sessions. Three essential elements characterise our textbooks for this purpose:

- An engaging and pleasant to read writing style—Textbooks impart knowledge. Putting this knowledge into words in such a way that readers enjoy it was our primary goal.
- Vividly developed case studies—In this textbook, we put our knowledge in a nutshell for you. Our case studies, which we hope will make you smile or even laugh, are supposed to translate abstract knowledge into comprehensible action in everyday situations.
- Immediate reflection on what has been learned—Communication is something every day. This means that communication is basically accessible to everyone at all times. In the course of reading our textbooks, we specifically encourage readers to experience and try out what they have just read in their environment.

We wish you an interesting and profitable read.

Ulf Lubienetzki
Hamburg, Germany

Heidrun Schüler-Lubienetzki
Hamburg, Germany
May 2020

Contents

1	**Introduction**	1
	References	3
2	**Facilitation?! What Is It?**	5
2.1	Basics, Terms and Definitions	6
2.2	Goals and Limits of Facilitation	8
2.3	Facilitation as a Process	12
	References	13
3	**More Than Two People Are Involved in the Facilitation Process**	15
3.1	The Contracting Authority	16
3.2	The Facilitator	18
3.2.1	Theme-Centred Interaction	18
3.2.2	Basic Attitude of the Facilitator	21
3.2.3	Role and Tasks of the Facilitator	22
3.3	The Group	23
	References	28
4	**Always One Step at a Time**	31
4.1	The Contract	33
4.2	The Preparation	35
4.3	The Facilitated Group Work	38
4.3.1	Start	38
4.3.2	Content Work	40
4.3.3	End	43
4.4	Follow-Up	43
	References	45
5	**Special Settings and Challenges of Facilitation**	47
5.1	Large Group Procedures	48
5.1.1	World Café	49
5.1.2	Open Space	50
5.2	Challenges and Pitfalls	52
5.2.1	Group Dynamic Effects at the Beginning of a Facilitated Session	52
5.2.2	Planning Replaces Chance with Error	53
5.2.3	Resistance in Groups	53
	References	57
6	**Overall Summary in Key Terms**	59
	References	63
	Supplementary Information	
	Glossary	66
	Index	69

About the Authors

Ulf Lubienetzki
has been working for several years as a consultant, business coach, and trainer with professionals and executives in various industries. In addition, he has more than 20 years of experience as a manager up to the executive level in various national and international management consulting firms. Ulf Lubienetzki holds a degree in engineering and studied social pedagogy and sociology. In the guidebooks and textbooks he has written, he brings his wide-ranging practical experience from working with his clients.

Heidrun Schüler-Lubienetzki
has been working as a business coach, leadership trainer, management consultant for more than two decades. Heidrun Schüler-Lubienetzki is a psychologist with a focus on personnel and organisational development as well as a talk therapist. In more than two decades, she has worked with several thousand specialists and executives up to the board level. As an author of guidebooks as well as specialists and textbooks, she passes on her knowledge and experience.

Both authors lead together the company entwicklung GbR in their coaching house in Hamburg-Rahlstedt. entwicklung GbR stands for
- coaching of specialists and managers
- individual and team training
- consulting for change processes in organisations

Together with its clients, entwicklung GbR works to maintain and increase the personal performance of specialists and managers, to develop high-performing and efficient teams, to reduce the waste of resources caused by dysfunctional conflicts, and to provide competent advice and goal-oriented support for change.

If you have any questions or need information about personal coaching, seminars, or training, you will find a wide range of information at ▶ http://www.entwicklung-hamburg.de

If you have any questions, feedback, or suggestions, please do not hesitate to contact us by e-mail: ▶ info@entwicklung-hamburg.de

Introduction

Contents

References – 3

© Springer-Verlag GmbH Germany, part of Springer Nature 2022
U. Lubienetzki, H. Schüler-Lubienetzki, *Tell Me, Where Are We Going and How Do We Get There?*,
https://doi.org/10.1007/978-3-662-65588-7_1

Let us start with some good news: the basics on human communication, which you can read about, for example, in the books "How we talk to each other" (Lubienetzki & Schüler-Lubienetzki, 2021a) and "Let's Talk with Each Other!" (Lubienetzki & Schüler-Lubienetzki, 2021b), also apply when more than two people, i.e. groups, communicate with each other. However, with an increasing number of people, the complexity of communication also increases. If we leave out all other factors, the mere consideration that every group member has a specific relationship to every other group member shows the extent of complexity. With five people there are already ten relationship combinations and with ten people there are 45 combinations—assuming, of course, that these persons in the relationships define their relationship in the same way. In order for groups to communicate successfully, there are various ways to support communication.

One way to deal with this complexity would certainly be to regulate communication very strictly. In this case, only what conforms to the rules would be communicated. One example is the very formal and regulated radiotelephony communication in the area of flight safety. Such a regulation ensures that everything in the communication that does not conform to the rules would be lost, which in turn would contradict the idea of constructive and creative cooperation between groups.

Another support option is to appoint a group leader. This person then has the task, among other things, of controlling the communication of the group members (e.g. in the meeting of a department). Depending on the design of the leadership function, this variant allows significantly more creativity and commitment of the group members than a strictly regulated cooperation. Nevertheless, there is a risk that the work results are very much determined by the person with the leadership function and that resources available in the group remain unused in the process.

However, in order to really be able to use all the knowledge and skills as well as all the experience available in a group, the group members should be free and equal in the content-related work. Facilitated cooperation offers such an opportunity. Facilitation, with its procedures and methods, aims to support the group process without restricting the content work of the group or imposing other requirements. The facilitator is neutral in terms of content and feels like a supporter or even service provider of the group's interests and its goal-oriented work.

You will realise in the course of this book that the terms presenter and facilitator are nowadays often used in an inflationary manner and not in accordance with the aforementioned understanding of the role. Television presenters who put their guests in a difficult situation, take centre stage themselves, promote their personal opinion, and are more concerned to entertain the viewers than to support their guests, are behaving contrary to the understanding of the role of a presenter. Surely this inexpedient understanding of the role will have its share in the fact that we as viewers often wonder what actually came out in the end in a political talk show—or that we know why nothing could come out.

Let us now look together at what facilitation is about, how to do a facilitation, and how groups manage different tasks and achieve goals that they could never have successfully worked on without support.

You can see an overview of the individual chapters of this book in ◘ Fig. 1.1.

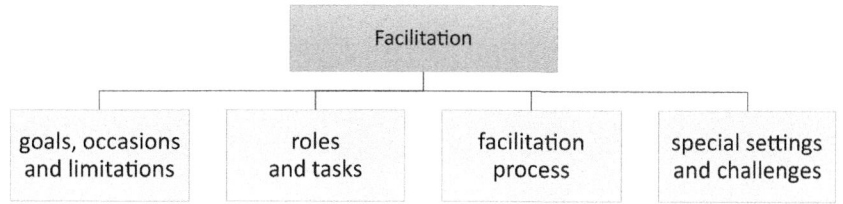

□ Fig. 1.1 The book at a glance

We will look at the topic of "facilitation" from different angles: first, we will have a look at the suitability of facilitation. In which situations is it the right method and when is it not suitable or even wrong? (▶ Chap. 2). Then, we will look at the various participants, their tasks (▶ Chap. 3), and the facilitation process (▶ Chap. 4). Finally, we discuss special formats and challenges (▶ Chap. 5).

References

Lubienetzki, U., & Schüler-Lubienetzki, H. (2021a). *How we talk to each other. The messages we send with our words and body language.* Springer.

Lubienetzki, U., & Schüler-Lubienetzki, H. (2021b). *Let's talk with each other! Psychology of successful conversation.* Springer.

Facilitation?! What Is It?

Definition, Goals and Limits of Facilitation

Contents

2.1 Basics, Terms and Definitions – 6

2.2 Goals and Limits of Facilitation – 8

2.3 Facilitation as a Process – 12

References – 13

© Springer-Verlag GmbH Germany, part of Springer Nature 2022
U. Lubienetzki, H. Schüler-Lubienetzki, *Tell Me, Where Are We Going and How Do We Get There?*,
https://doi.org/10.1007/978-3-662-65588-7_2

Even when two people communicate with each other, the conversation process can be very complex. When a group of people communicates, the complexity increases significantly. In professional contexts in particular, it is commonplace for groups to have to work together in a targeted manner. The range of groups found in companies extends from strictly regulated working relationships to very free expert groups that are supposed to solve a problem together. The fewer rules are set up for the cooperation, the higher the need for communication and the complexity of the cooperation. Facilitation opens up the opportunity to support and enable groups to work together in a goal-oriented manner and to master the communicative complexity.

After reading this chapter in depth, you will be able to ...
- **Define** what is meant by facilitation.
- State the **objectives** of facilitation.
- Explain under which **circumstances** facilitation is the appropriate approach.
- Identify the **problems** that can arise in group work.
- Explain which steps make up the **facilitation process.**

2.1 Basics, Terms and Definitions

There are terms that we encounter almost every day. **Facilitation** and the associated person, the *facilitator*, are certainly such terms. For example, facilitator in the professional environment there are facilitated workshops, meetings, working groups and much more can be found. Managers are not only supposed to lead; they are supposed to be facilitators for their team. Conflicts are also dealt with in a facilitated way. The list could certainly be continued.

If we ask about the meaning of the word *facilitation* in this context, the definitions are similarly diverse, as the following compilation of quotations shows:

1. Facilitation is the observation and stimulation of the development of communication as well as reflection on the forms of perception and interactions in groups of decision-makers in order to use the resources available to cope with complexity as well as to regulate conflicts that arise, with the aim of making joint and appropriate decisions and establishing collective capacity to act (Freimuth, 2010, pp. 4–5).
2. The method of facilitation is a craft, an art of making the conversation between people meaningful and productive (Klebert et al., 2002, p. 15).
3. Facilitation is an approach that can be used to structure communication in groups in such a way that the resources of all participants are made available to the group's work process in an optimal way. Through the participation of all participants in decision-making, goal-setting and implementation, a high degree of identification of the participants with the goals to be aimed is achieved. (Graeßner, 2008, p. 9)

2.1 · Basics, Terms and Definitions

4. Facilitation is a method used to support working groups in working on a topic, a problem or a task,
   - focused on the content, purposeful and efficient,
   - self-reliant,
   - dealing with each other satisfactorily and as trouble-free as possible
   - as well as oriented towards the implementation in everyday practice. (Hartmann et al., 1999, p. 16)

Whether facilitation is an art, a craft, an approach or a method is, in our opinion, not the main issue. From our point of view, the definition does not have to contain anything about the contents of facilitation (e.g., making resources available, regulating conflicts or dealing with topics and tasks). In our view, the following short definition, based on the above-mentioned definitions, describes the core of facilitation:

> **Definition**
>
> **Facilitation** purposefully supports the communication of people in groups (see Freimuth, 2010; Klebert et al., 2002; Graeßner, 2008; Hartmann et al., 1999).

Analogous to Graeßner (2008), we understand facilitation as a process, for which the facilitator is responsible. The content of the work results is the responsibility of the (working) group (Graeßner, 2008; Funcke & Havenith, 2010). By analogy with a chemical reaction, Funcke and Havenith (2010) state: Facilitation has a catalytic effect (p. 12). Graeßner (2008) also refers to the facilitators a **catalyst** of the group process (p. 24).

> **Definition**
>
> A **catalyst** is "a substance that causes or speeds a chemical reaction without itself being changed." (Cambridge University Press, n.d.)

The methodological foundations of facilitation have been laid in the late 1960s. It was about successful communication in groups of decision-makers and experts who had to solve increasingly complex challenges together (Freimuth, 2010).

The five axioms of human communication by Watzlawick et al. (1968) also apply in groups. The resulting extended communication model applies to the entire group and to any combination of two group members (Watzlawick et al., 1968). Consequently, the possibilities of misunderstandings, disruptions, or conflicts, and thus their probability of occurrence, increase with the size of the group. In the further course of this book, we will also relate to the basics of human communication and the conduct of conversations (see Lubienetzki & Schüler-Lubienetzki, 2021a, 2021b).

Facilitation is a way of supporting human communication in groups in a targeted manner and thus shaping it successfully. Before we look at how the facilitation process works in detail, we will get to the bottom of the question of which objectives can realistically be achieved with facilitation and where facilitation has its limits.

2.2 Goals and Limits of Facilitation

Communication is successful when its objective is achieved. In this context, facilitation has the goal of successfully shaping communication in groups. However, besides facilitation, there are other ways to support communication in groups (e.g., leadership or counselling). However, let us first look at the challenges of communication in groups in more detail. We will then discuss the question of when facilitation is suitable for dealing with these challenges and when other supportive methods are more likely to be effective.

Following Freimuth (2010), groups face different communicative **challenges**:
1. Since only one participant can speak at a time, the opportunities to **contribute** are limited. In less structured discussions, up to 60 verbal contributions per hour are possible. The more demanding and conflictual the topic is, the longer the individual contributions become and fewer contributions are possible in an hour. The resources of silent participants are not used in such situations.
2. Unstructured and non-visualised contributions can lead to the "**common thread**" being lost or getting lost inside discussions. Each participant has their own attitude, interests and agenda. This increases the risk of certain individuals dominating the discussion and focusing mainly on their topics.
3. **Reluctant** or even new participants are less likely to have their say. Their personality or even a lack of knowledge makes it difficult for them to join in.
4. The **results** of the discussion can be lost without appropriate documentation. (Partisan) participants could document the discussion results biased towards their respective attitude and evaluation.
5. The **creative potential** of groups could not be harnessed. Different knowledge as well as different experiences and perspectives are only available to a very limited extent in unstructured and undocumented discussions.
6. **Decision-making** in groups could be blocked in the discussion. Especially when it is important that many different points of view and ideas are first collected and in a second step evaluated, there is a high risk for polarisation and discussions about the positions of certain group members. Conflicts could break out and the ability to reach agreement would be limited or lost altogether.
7. Similar to decision-making, **agreement processes** in groups can escalate and become conflicts on the one hand, or on the other hand lead to one part of the group claiming opinion leadership and the rest behaving passively. If the passivity in the group does not result from acceptance, the lack of acceptance will probably break through at a later point in time.

2.2 · Goals and Limits of Facilitation

Many of the challenges mentioned by Freimuth could probably be met by a person taking over the leadership of the group. However, a formal or even informal leadership creates other problems, which are presented as follows, based on Graeßner (2008):

1. The discussion is often **dominated** by the leader. The participants try to fulfil the expectations of the leaders—regardless of the extent to which they actually support decisions. A feeling of powerlessness arises in them; their own ideas are not brought up in the group, but in other constellations (e.g., in the subsequent hallway conversation).
2. Discussions are also cut short in the face of resistance by the leaders announcing **decisions**. As a result, results lack comprehensibility and acceptance. Ideas and further potential are also lost if the knowledge and experience of parts of the group remain unused.

> **Case Study**
>
> Mr. Wilson was confronted by his managing director John Smith with his derogatory behaviour towards the trainees. At first he could not understand the criticism, but eventually Mr. Wilson admitted that his behavior could be interpreted as slightly dismissive at one point or another. As a possibility to improve the cooperation with the trainees in the future, both agreed that Mr. Wilson would organise a meeting with the trainees in which the future cornerstones of the cooperation should be developed.
>
> So Mr. Wilson called the trainees together the next day. Beforehand, he had thought carefully about what he wanted. Certain rules had to be in place. These included that the trainees kept order, were punctual and fulfilled their tasks as he instructed them. The conversational tone could certainly be friendlier—he would get his act together. He also wanted to ask the trainees what suggestions they had for better cooperation.
>
> The meeting went as Mr. Wilson had planned. He made his points. The trainees agreed with him or did not contradict him. They did not seem to have any new or additional suggestions, at least nobody said anything. All in all, the whole thing took less than half an hour. "Really efficient," thought Mr. Wilson. Following the meeting, he was glad the subject was over. He did find it a little odd that some of the trainees had said nothing at all. But he had asked several times and everyone had had their chance.
>
> When Mr. Wilson told his manager about the meeting, John Smith was not as pleased as he was. Afterwards, he wondered what John Smith meant when he said "Maybe we'll get further with a facilitator." "After all, I led the trainees through the meeting according to plan, so what do we need a facilitator for?" he thought.

? Reflection Task

Please put yourself in the trainees' shoes and answer the following questions: How would you have felt in the position of a trainee in this situation? What would you have wished for in the meeting in order to shape the future cooperation? How should Mr. Wilson have behaved?

Let us now systematically examine when facilitation is the appropriate means in order to support communication in groups. You will see that there can be good reasons to use to use a variant of leadership in groups like Mr. Wilson did. However, in the example given with the objective of involving the trainees, it was obviously not very appropriate.

Adapted from Graeßner (2008) and Freimuth (2010), facilitation has the following **objectives** when working with groups:
1. Making **decisions**—transparency and agreement on and selection of alternative courses of action
2. Support **communication**—targeted promotion of exchange as well as handling of conflicts
3. Use existing **potentials**—stimulate creativity and integrate knowledge and competences
4. Promote motivation and **satisfaction**—find joint solutions and develop results

Freimuth mentions other possibilities and concepts besides facilitation to support group work in a targeted manner. Depending on the degree of complexity of the tasks to be accomplished and the degree to which the group members are affected, decisions can be made by leaders, project management, conflict management, and change management (Freimuth, 2010, p. 10) (see ◘ Fig. 2.1).

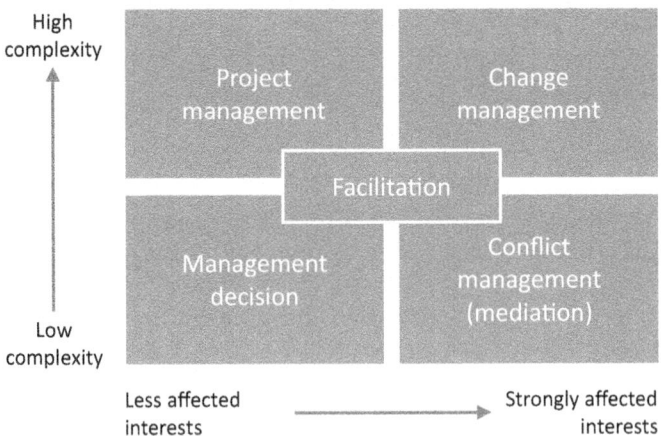

◘ **Fig. 2.1** Possibilities and concepts for supporting work in groups. Facilitation is the means to use when it is about tasks with a medium level of complexity and when the group members' interests are moderately affected. Extreme manifestations of the areas can usually be dealt with more effectively in other ways or with other methods. (Source: Own representation based on Freimuth, 2010, p. 10)

Facilitation always reaches its limits when the complexity of the problem to be solved is very high and/or the interests of the group members are very strongly affected. If the complexity is high, the **management** of a problem or task (e.g., the preparation of a complex decision on how to proceed in the context of project or change management) is required first.

Definition

Management can generally be understood "as the process of planning, organizing, directing, and controlling the activities of employees in combination with other resources to accomplish organizational objectives." (Black & Bright, 2019).

If the degree of complexity and the degree of involvement are rather low, the manager can decide and inform the group members about their decision or give appropriate work instructions. If the degree of involvement is high and the complexity is low, conflicts are likely and need to be managed (Freimuth, 2010).

Graeßner (2008) also points out that facilitation is no panacea (p. 19) and notes that the working environment and working conditions cannot be influenced by facilitation. A very pronounced hierarchical structure, a conflict-prone or even an unsafe working environment are examples that work against the successful use of facilitation (Graeßner, 2008).

Even if the prerequisites for the successful use of facilitation are given, there is no guarantee of success. Communication can fail for various reasons. For example, the relationship between people may be unclear or disturbed, personal attitudes to each other or to the topic may be conducive or inhibiting, or people may enter into resistance for different personal motives (see Lubienetzki & Schüler-Lubienetzki, 2021a, 2021b).

Ultimately, the competence of the facilitator as well as the knowledge and competences of the group are limiting factors for facilitated cooperation in groups. In this context, Freimuth points to problem areas that can be traced back to the core of the aforementioned communication disturbances (Freimuth, 2010, pp. 23–24):

1. **"Suboptimal use of information"**
   The focus of the exchange is on information known to all participants. The knowledge of individuals is used only hesitantly.
2. **"Group Think"**
   Excessive striving for consensus with the effect that the group overestimates itself and reacts narrow-mindedly and with social pressure to dissenting opinions.
3. **"Entrapment"**
   In late stages of decision-making—after a lot of personal commitment has already been invested by the group and each individual—the group is trapped in its previous results. It is unwilling to admit mistakes despite disadvantages and stubbornly sticks to the chosen path.
4. **"Decision Autism"**
   The group strives to validate itself and closes its eyes to other options.

? Reflection Task

Please think about your own experiences in connection with facilitated groups. Have there been sessions where the outcome of the work fell short of your expectations? Please examine such an experience in more detail. What could have been the reason that the outcome did not meet your expectations?

2.3 Facilitation as a Process

At the beginning of this book we looked at different definitions of facilitation. Various authors refer to facilitation as an *art*, a *craft,* an *approach*, or a *method.* According to our proposed definition, facilitation supports goal-oriented communication in groups. It assists the group on its way to its goal and can therefore, in our view, be seen as a supportive **process**. The process begins with the decision to facilitate and ends with the conclusion of the facilitation and its follow-up.

We base our process steps in ◘ Fig. 2.2 on a four-step process of planning, preparation, facilitation and follow-up of facilitation according to Freimuth (2010, p. 61):

The facilitation process is carried out by three participants. The client decides for facilitation and concludes the contract with the facilitator. The facilitator pre-

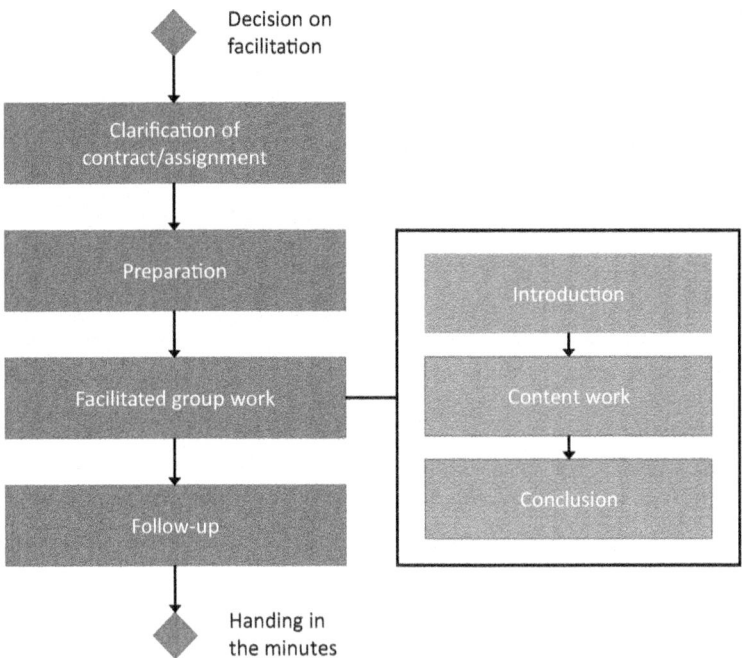

◘ **Fig. 2.2** The facilitation process. The facilitation process consists of the four steps "clarification of the contract or the assignment", "preparation of the facilitation", the facilitation itself and the follow-up of the facilitation. The process starts with the decision for facilitation and usually ends with the submission of the minutes (see Freimuth, 2010, p. 61)

pares for the facilitated session. Then the actual facilitated group work follows, in which the facilitator works with the group on the topics or the problem. Finally, the facilitator does the follow-up work of the facilitation and submits a protocol.

So much for the first overview of the process. In Chap. ▶ 3, we will deal with the process participants and in Chap. ▶ 4 we will go into detail about the individual process steps.

> **Summary in Key Terms**
> - We encounter facilitation in various situations in everyday life. The definitions of facilitation are just as **diverse.**
> - In this book, **facilitation** refers to the *targeted support* of communication in *groups*. The facilitator shapes the **process** but does *not* interfere with the *content*.
>   - The facilitator can be compared to a **catalyst** in their role.
> - Facilitation **enables** groups to *solve* problems and conflicts and to *reflect on* their own work and interaction (Freimuth, 2010).
> - Facilitation is **used when** ...
>   - it is about making *decisions* in groups, *supporting* communication, using *potentials* and promoting *motivation* and satisfaction (Freimuth, 2010; Graeßner, 2008).
>   - the *degree of complexity of* the topics to be dealt with and the degree to which the participants are *affected* are in the middle range. If the complexity and/or the degree of involvement are high, **management** is an alternative. If there is little complexity and/or involvement, management or mediation may be more effective (Freimuth, 2010).
> - The **success** of facilitation is influenced by the working conditions and environment of the group members, by communication disturbances that may occur, and by the competences of the facilitator and the group members.
>   - Problems that can occur during group work are suboptimal use of information, group think, entrapment, or decision autism.
> - The **facilitation process** can be divided into several steps (Freimuth, 2010; Funcke & Havenith, 2010):
>   1. The *clarification of the contract or assignment* by the client and the facilitator.
>   2. *Preparation of* the facilitator for the group work.
>   3. *Support of* the group's *working process* by the facilitator.
>   4. The *follow-up of* the group work by the facilitator.

References

Black, J. S., & Bright, D. S. (2019). *Organizational behavior*. OpenStax. Retrieved September 15, 2021, from https://openstax.org/books/organizational-behavior/pages/1-3-the-nature-of-management

Cambridge University Press. (n.d.). Catalyst. In *Cambridge Academic Content Dictionary*. Retrieved September 8, 2021, from https://dictionary.cambridge.org/dictionary/english/catalyst

Freimuth, J. (2010). *Moderation [Facilitation]*. Hogrefe.

Funcke, A., & Havenith, E. (2010). *Moderations-Tools. Anschauliche, aktivierende und klärende Methoden für die Moderations-Praxis [Facilitation tools. Illustrative, activating and clarifying methods for facilitation practice]*. ManagerSeminare.

Graeßner, G. (2008). *Moderation—das Lehrbuch [Facilitation—the textbook]*. Ziel.

Hartmann, M., Rieger, M., & Luoma, M. (1999). *Zielgerichtet moderieren. Ein Handbuch für Führungskräfte, Berater und Trainer [Facilitating purposefully. A handbook for managers, consultants and trainers]* (2nd ed.). Beltz.

Klebert, K., Schrader, E., & Straub, W. (2002). *Moderations-Methode. Das Standardwerk [Facilitation method. The standard work]*. Windmühle.

Lubienetzki, U., & Schüler-Lubienetzki, H. (2016). *Sag mal: Wo geht's lang und wie kommen wir dahin? Moderation [Tell me: Which way is it and how do we get there? Facilitation]* (Study letter of the Fresenius University of Applied Sciences online plus GmbH). Hochschule Fresenius online plus GmbH.

Lubienetzki, U., & Schüler-Lubienetzki, H. (2021a). *How we talk to each other. The messages we send with our words and body language*. Springer.

Lubienetzki, U., & Schüler-Lubienetzki, H. (2021b). *Let's talk with each other! Psychology of successful conversation*. Springer.

Watzlawick, P., Beavin, J. H., & Jackson, D. D. (1968). *Pragmatics of human communication. A study of interactional patterns, pathologies, and paradoxes*. Faber and Faber.

More Than Two People Are Involved in the Facilitation Process

Roles in the Facilitation Process

Contents

3.1 The Contracting Authority – 16

3.2 The Facilitator – 18
3.2.1 Theme-Centred Interaction – 18
3.2.2 Basic Attitude of the Facilitator – 21
3.2.3 Role and Tasks of the Facilitator – 22

3.3 The Group – 23

References – 28

© Springer-Verlag GmbH Germany, part of Springer Nature 2022
U. Lubienetzki, H. Schüler-Lubienetzki, *Tell Me, Where Are We Going and How Do We Get There?*,
https://doi.org/10.1007/978-3-662-65588-7_3

Three roles or participants belong to facilitation: one person defines the assignment (the client), another facilitates (the facilitator), and the group does the substantive work.

After reading this chapter in-depth, you will be able to ...
- Identify the issues that a **client** should consider before deciding to undertake facilitation.
- Explain what is meant by the concept of theme-centered **interaction** (TCI) according to Ruth Cohn (1980).
  - Reflect on the three central **factors of** TCI and describe their role in the facilitation process.
- Derive **rules** for the **attitude** and **behaviour** of the facilitator and the group members based on TCI.
- Define the **role** and associated **tasks of** a **facilitator**.
- Analyse the **structure of working groups**.
- Recognise in which **development phase** a group is.
- Differentiate different **roles** within a **group**.

3.1 The Contracting Authority

> **Case Study**
>
> John Smith was not at all satisfied with Mr. Wilson's "workshop". As far as he understood, Mr. Wilson had made his view of good cooperation clear to the trainees and the trainees had silently taken note of his suggestions. A genuine debate and joint decision-making had not even begun to take place. His spontaneously expressed decision was clear: with the help of a facilitator, a "real" workshop should be held with the trainees.

The most important task of the client is to make the decision about the implementation of facilitation and to commission the facilitator. In order to be able to make this decision, the client should clarify to what extent the topics and problems to be discussed are suitable for facilitation, whether facilitation fits the corporate and work culture, what the goals of facilitation are and what room for manoeuvre the group has. If there is clarity about these questions, the only thing missing is the facilitator. The requirements for facilitation are to be formulated and based on these the suitable facilitator is selected (Freimuth, 2010).

Let us take a closer look at the preparatory questions of the **client,** following Freimuth (2010) and Hartmann et al. (1999):
1. **Suitability of the topic**
   Facilitation in the cooperation of groups means that work is done in an open-ended manner. The solution emerges in the facilitated group process.

Therefore, topics whose solution allows for more room for manoeuvre are particularly suitable for facilitation. Since all group members are involved in the solution, more information is available. Basically, all group members are to be involved in the process, so that the processing of the information requires an appropriate contingent of time. In a nutshell: the more room for manoeuvre, the more information and the longer the time horizon, the more suitable a topic is for facilitation.

2. **Fit with the corporate and work culture**
Facilitation means that a group is given greater scope for action and decision-making or, conversely, that individual decision-makers explicitly relinquish power. In the group, all participants have equal rights—formal or hierarchical positions have no significance in facilitated groups. Finally, the group must have sufficient time to work on the problems. In a nutshell: The culture of the organisation should allow for decision-makers to relinquish power and for decisions to actually be taken by the group, as well as for group members to have equal rights and sufficient time.

3. **Determination of objectives and scope for action**
Facilitation is the goal-oriented support of cooperation in groups. In order for facilitation to be effective, the client must define the goals of the group's work. It is important to outline the topic in sufficient detail and to specify the criteria for when the goals have been achieved. In addition, the facilitator and the group need some room for manoeuvre, which should be sufficiently large. The limits should be set in such a way that there is actually a chance of finding a solution within this framework. Thus, the room for manoeuvre can range from the mere collection of ideas to the development of various solution scenarios to the formulating a decision.

The **selection** of the facilitator is the client's task. In the following section, we will take a closer look at the role, the qualifications, and the personal attitude of the facilitator. The decision on the person can be based on this outline.

> ▶ **Example: Is Facilitation Appropriate for My Situation?**
> - John Smith decided to review his "gut decision" on facilitation:
> - He was concerned that Mr. Wilson should work together with the trainees to shape the cooperation.
> - John Smith was prepared to give the trainees sufficient room for manoeuvre in this respect.
> - He also wanted to talk intensively with Mr. Wilson before the workshop and make it clear to him that he was not in charge in the facilitated group process but could contribute on an equal footing. This would be a difficult undertaking, but he was aware that the group process would only be successful if Mr. Wilson adjusted his attitude accordingly.
> - In order not to make the first step too big, ideas should first be collected and initial options for action should be identified. A decision should only be made in the second step.

- Employment contract basics, such as remuneration or working hours were not included in the room for manoeuvre.
- Otherwise, the group should be free to work.
- He also already knew one facilitator: his younger sister Amy Smith. She had both mediator and facilitator training and John Smith knew that she had already worked wonders in other companies. ◄

3.2 The Facilitator

The facilitator supports the group in working on the content in a goal-oriented manner. In doing so, the facilitator places themselves completely at the service of the group. The topic-centered interaction described below helps the facilitator to understand how communication and cooperation in the group can be shaped in a goal-oriented and ultimately successful way. This understanding helps the facilitator to adapt their attitude as well as behaviour to the group work and to fulfil the expectations of the facilitator's role.

3.2.1 Theme-Centred Interaction

In order to understand which personal attitude is goal-oriented when working with groups, we would first like to look at goal-oriented work in groups. Ruth Cohn began to develop a method for this in the mid-1950s: **theme-centered interaction**, or **TCI** for short (Cohn, 1980).

The term *"theme-centered interaction"*, which may sound rather unwieldy to some, was chosen very deliberately by Ruth Cohn, since the method is about placing the theme or the task at the center of the attention of each and every participant and then working on the theme together with everyone, i.e. in interaction with each other (Langmaak, 1991).

The basic model of theme-centered interaction consists of **three factors**, which could be pictured as the vertices of a triangle: (1) I, the personality; (2) we, the group; (3) it, the theme. This triangle is embedded in a sphere that represents the **environment** in which the interactional group meets, the so-called globe. This environment consists of time, place, and their historical, social, and teleological circumstances (Cohn, 1980, p. 113). This results in the picture in ◘ Fig. 3.1.

The basic working hypothesis of theme-centered interaction is that in the cooperation and interaction of groups the three factors "theme", "I", and "we"—placed in the context of the globe—have equal importance. Throughout the entire process of interaction, the three factors should be evenly balanced. Thus, there are phases in the interaction in which one factor is particularly emphasised but over the entire period of interaction, the balance is restored. Everything that takes

3.2 · The Facilitator

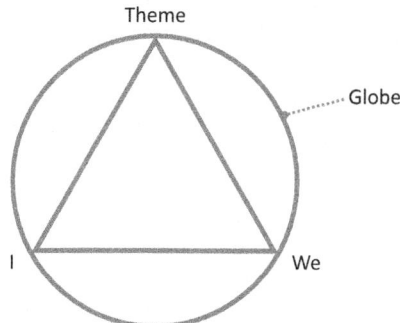

Fig. 3.1 The triangle of theme-centered interaction. The triangle of theme-centered interaction expresses that "theme", "I" and "we" are equal in group processes and should be addressed in a balanced way. The globe ensures that the outcomes of the group process fit into the reality of the group. (Source: own representation based on Cohn, 1980, pp. 113–114)

place in the interaction of the group, in the ego of each individual, and in relation to the topic must fit the globe. Not including the globe substantially increases the risk of working out unsuitable and unrealistic results (Cohn, 1980; Langmaak, 1991).

> **Important**
> Figuratively we can imagine the balancing in TCI in such a way that the triangle is placed in its centre of gravity on a needle. The corners are given different weights throughout the group process. If the triangle tilts in one direction, the weight must be shifted to other corners in order to restore balance.

Ruth Cohn formulated this:

When I lead a group, I try to keep an eye on each participant as well as the group as a whole and the topic, without ignoring my feelings and thoughts. I observe and balance the group process. If the group becomes over-intellectual, I speak of my feelings; if it responds only emotionally, I establish balance through my reflections and factual discussion; if the group speaks only to the topic, I pay attention to the group process and the expression and behaviour of individuals (Cohn, 1980, p. 118).

The basic model of theme-centered Interaction with the three factors "theme", "I", "we", and the globe is brought to life by people. In the world of theme-centered interaction, people are as dependent on independence as they are on connectedness with other people. In this context, each person is absolutely to be valued and respected. After all, every person has limits which they can expand (Cohn, 1980).

Derived from this axiomatic view of the human being are two basic **postulates** (Cohn, 1980; Langmaak, 1991):

» Be your own chairperson. (Cohn, 1980, p. 121)

This postulate means that every person first accepts themselves with their personality, their strengths, and weaknesses, their feelings, their limits as well as everything else that makes a person individual. There is no right and wrong. In their individuality a human being is dependent on other people. Furthermore, an individual is capable of developing beyond their present limitations in the future. They make their own decision about everything that concerns them.

» Disturbances take precedence. (Cohn, 1980, p. 122)

Disturbances are anything that impedes or prevents cooperation in the group. Disturbances are real and are therefore to be noticed and not ignored, they are to be recognised as human and dealt with because they have an obvious or subliminal negative influence on the group process. However, persistent causes of disturbance in individual people cannot always be countered in the group situation. In these cases, the group and its work have priority. The disruptive individual in these cases should deal with the cause of the disturbance outside the group. The maxim 'Reality takes precedence.' helps to make decisions about precedence; it takes practice not to abuse this 'danger rule.' (Cohn, 1980, p. 123).

> **Definition**
>
> A **postulate** is "a hypothesis advanced as an essential presupposition, condition, or premise of a train of reasoning" (Merriam-Webster, n.d.).

Theme-centered interaction is closely oriented to the practice of group work. The most important aspects of the individual's attitude and behaviour in group interaction are summarised in nine **auxiliary rules** (Cohn, 1980, pp. 124–128):
1. Represent yourself in your statements, saying 'I', not 'we' or 'one'.
2. If you ask a question, say why you ask and what this question means to you. Reveal yourself as a person and avoid an interview.
3. Be authentic and selective in your communications. Be aware of what you think and feel, and choose what you say and do.
4. Restrain yourself as long as possible in interpreting others. Speak of your personal reactions instead.
5. Be cautious about generalisations.
6. If you make a statement concerning another participant's behaviour or characteristics, also say what it means to you that they are the way they are (i.e., the way you see them).
7. Side discussions take precedence. They are disturbing and usually important. They wouldn't happen if they weren't important (Maybe you want to tell us what you're talking about with each other?).
8. Only one person speaks at a time.
9. If more persons want to speak at the same time, tell each other in key words what you intend to talk about.

3.2 · The Facilitator

❓ Reflection Task
Please have another look at the postulates and auxiliary rules of TCI. Now, think of a workshop or a meeting that you have facilitated yourself or that was facilitated by another person. Please find examples from this workshop or meeting in which the postulates and auxiliary rules were acted upon. How did this play out? Were there also meetings in which the postulates and auxiliary rules were not followed? What were the consequences?

3.2.2 Basic Attitude of the Facilitator

Personal attitude in facilitation is identical with **attitude**, which Triandis (1975) understands as "an idea charged with emotion which predisposes a class of actions to a particular class of social situations" (p. 4; see also Lubienetzki & Schüler-Lubienetzki, 2021). Especially in facilitated group work, where the facilitator communicates with the group and at the same time supports the communication in the group, the personal attitude is of particular importance. The facilitator is dependent on getting in touch with the group and building a relationship that enables purposeful collaboration.

Theme-centered interaction is based on the **human image** that axiomatically assumes that every human being is to be treated appreciatively and respectfully. Furthermore, every human being is, on the one hand, independent and, on the other hand, dependent on social connectedness. After all, every person is capable of expanding their boundaries (Cohn, 1980).

This human image should underlie the facilitator's attitude. Based on Freimuth (2010), Graeßner (2008) and Klebert et al. (2002) the following attributes describe the **personal attitude** of the facilitator:

1. **Appreciative, respectful, and approvingly**
   In order to get into contact with the group and each person in it, it is essential to meet them with appreciation, respect, and also recognition. Only if contact is established on this basis, the content-related work can be supported in a targeted manner.
2. **Involving the whole person**
   People interact factually and emotionally. Emotions are not a hindrance but release energy to solve the problems at hand. The goal is to activate and use all resources of the individual as well as the group.
3. **Helping and supporting**
   The facilitator places themselves entirely at the service of the group. The result of the work is the success of the group; the fact that the group has reached the result is the success of the facilitator.
4. **Neutral**
   Each opinion and each result produced by the group is legitimate. The facilitator does not evaluate or judge. There is neither a right nor a wrong for them.

5. **Responsible and encouraging self-responsibility**
   The facilitator is aware of their limits and deals with them responsibly. They encourage the group to deal with their boundaries in the same responsible way.
6. **Questioning**
   Curiosity and genuine interest in the facilitator's questions arouse the group's attention and promote communication. Not only one but individually different answers and opinions are welcome.
7. **Clarifying and solving**
   Everything that happens in the group has meaning. This also includes disturbances in particular. The facilitator recognises conflicts and problems, makes them transparent, and works towards their solution.

> **Case Study**
>
> John Smith wondered why he immediately thought of his younger sister when he thought of the role of facilitator to be filled. Even at school, his sister had a talent for settling disputes between classmates. Interestingly, she never did so with a raised finger, as some teachers do but by speaking kindly and appreciatively to the disputants. Somehow, she always managed to calm down even the most heated tempers and talk objectively about the conflict. She treated everyone equally. She never took sides but asked questions and helped both sides to find a compromise on their own.
>
> Today, she had turned this talent into a profession. She was a mediator and a gifted facilitator. Even in tricky situations, she was able to treat her clients with respect and appreciation and build trust with all parties involved. John Smith was certain that Amy Smith could also help Mr. Wilson and his team to work together constructively.

3.2.3 Role and Tasks of the Facilitator

The personal attitude outlined in the previous section forms the foundation on which the facilitator works with the group. There is a clear difference in responsibilities between the facilitator and the group. In short, the facilitator is responsible for the path to the goal, the work process; the group is, or the group members are, responsible for contributing their knowledge and competence and producing sustainable results in terms of content (Funcke & Havenith, 2010).

In this context, the facilitator functions as a problem solver, conflict solver, and reflector (Freimuth, 2010). These three **role components** differ—based on Freimuth (2010), Funcke and Havenith (2010), Graeßner (2008), and Hartmann et al. (1999)—as follows:
1. In the role of **problem solver,** the facilitator initiates the discussion in the group. They purposefully involve all group members in the work process and help the group to use all the resources at its disposal. They keep an eye on the goal, create structure, and help the group to work in a goal-oriented way. By visualising

intermediate results, they ensure a uniform level of knowledge, systematises and secures the results of the work.
2. As a **conflict solver,** the facilitator proposes "game rules" for the joint work and makes sure that the rules agreed upon in the group are adhered to. The facilitator makes disturbances transparent and supports the processing of these disturbances. They make differences in opinions and interests transparent and suggest ways of reaching an agreement. Requests for change are solved by them in the group. Every participant is heard and included.
3. As a **reflector,** the facilitator shares their perceptions with the group as feedback. They also develop and promote the ability to give and receive feedback in the group. They pay attention to disturbing or blocking patterns in communication and reflect them. They direct the group's attention away from themselves towards the process and allow the group to consciously experience their collaboration and success.

Reflection Task
In a professional context, team meetings are usually chaired by the responsible manager. In some cases, the manager formulates that they would like to act as a facilitator in the meeting. Please consider up to which point the role of the manager can be combined with the role and tasks of the facilitator.

3.3 The Group

The group is of crucial importance in facilitated collaboration. It, or rather each member, bears the responsibility for contributing the available information and expertise and, in the end, for producing results that are viable in terms of content (Funcke & Havenith, 2010).

This gives the composition of the group a special significance. Since cooperation in the group is ultimately nothing other than communication, the relationship level is at least as important as the factual level in the discussion. So on the factual level the discussion might be about personal resources (including expertise, skills, information) while on the relationship level it is about the relationships among the participants (see Watzlawick et al., 1968).

The group as a whole, i.e. in its temporal and content-related structure, is also important. The range extends from a randomly formed group (e.g. in the context of a workshop at a large specialist conference) to a well-established team (e.g. a project team that has already been working together successfully for some time). The **temporal dimension** is characterised by the phases of group development and the **content dimension** by the different roles in the group (Gellert & Nowak, 2014).

For the facilitation, this means that the group and its members should be analysed in advance. The objective of such an analysis is to prepare the facilitation in such a way that it meets the needs of the group in the best possible way (Freimuth, 2010).

Following Freimuth (2010) and Gellert and Nowak (2014), the following questions about the analysis of the group should be answered in advance:
1. **Organisational embedding:**
    How do the participants relate to each other in the organisation? Is there a hierarchical divide (e.g. supervisor-employee relationship)? Which different organisational areas do the participants belong to?
2. **Resources:**
    What information and what expertise do the participants have? What experience do they have with (facilitated) group work?
3. **Interests:**
    Where do the participants agree on their interests? Where not? What is their perception of the topic? What is their attitude? Are there hopes or fears?
4. **Relationships:**
    Are there informal leaders? Are there unresolved conflicts or conflicts from the past with relevance to the topic? What other relationships of the participants are important?

In already established groups and teams, the phase the group is in as well as the different roles of the members can be analysed in more detail in advance of the facilitation. To systematise this, we take a look at two **models** that characterise the group phase on the one hand and the different roles within the group on the other:

- **Phases of Group Development**

In 1965, Tuckman presented a model for the development of groups. This model is based on four phases of group development, which are entitled "forming", "storming", "norming" and "performing" (Tuckman, 1965). These phases of a group's development are always passed through and can be visualised by means of a clock. Each quarter of the clock represents a phase. The forming phase can also be referred to as the "orientation phase", the storming phase as the "position-finding phase" or the "debate phase", the norming phase as the "organisation phase" or the "familiarity phase", and the performing phase as the "working phase" or the "phase of constructive cooperation" (Gellert & Nowak, 2014) (see ◘ Fig. 3.2).

❓ Reflection Task
You certainly belong to different groups at the moment. Please select a professional and a private group and determine in which group phase the respective group is currently. How is the cooperation or the interaction in the group and how do the group members behave? What has changed compared to earlier group phases?

- **Roles Within the Group**

In well performing groups or teams, certain roles are pronounced among the members. Each role does not necessarily have to be performed by different members. It

3.3 · The Group

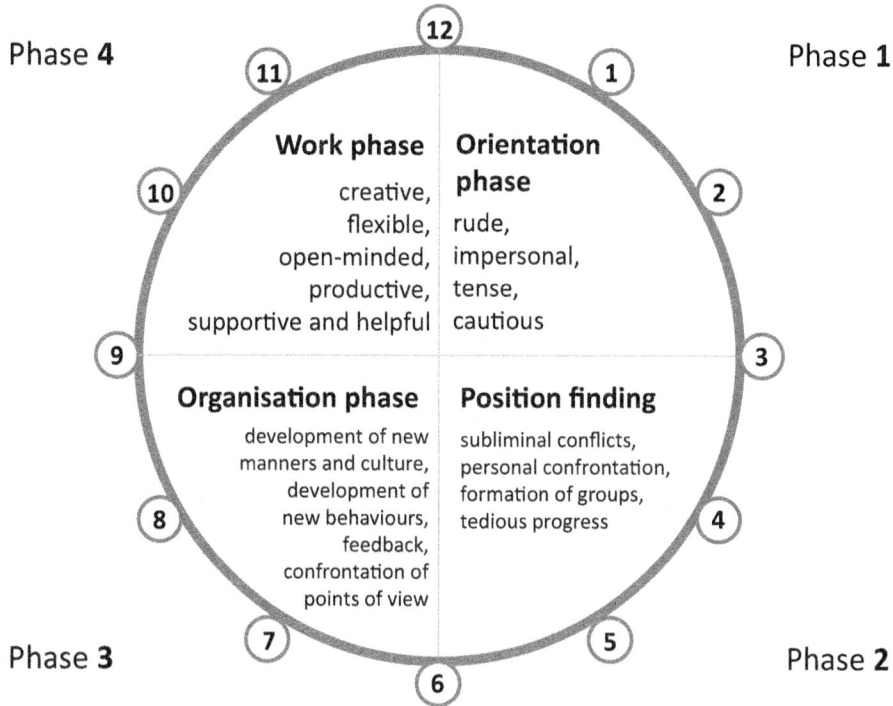

☐ **Fig. 3.2** Phases of group development with characterisation. The image of the "clock" shows the different phases of group development that are passed through in the course of cooperation: (1) the orientation phase, (2) the position-finding phase, (3) the organisation phase, and (4) the work phase. (Source: own representation based on Gellert & Nowak, 2014, p. 215)

is just as possible for one member to take on several roles. Gellert and Nowak's model assumes six roles that should be represented in well-functioning groups and teams (Gellert & Nowak, 2014, p. 72):

1. **Leader/facilitator**
   Often the role of the group leader results from the role within the organisation surrounding the group. Otherwise, the person who takes on this role is chosen by the group. Also, in the facilitating manifestation of this role, the role can be filled by either a member of the group or somebody external. The most important task of this role is to lead the group process in a more guiding way and to support it in a more facilitating way.

2. **Implementer/coordinator**
   This role is behind the leader/facilitator role and holds the technical content leadership. The role can be developed to the extent that the informal leadership of the group is taken over. The most important task is to give the collaboration a realistic structure focused on implementation.

3. **Creative generator of ideas**

   This role suggests new paths, has a wealth of new ideas, and is prepared to leave the beaten track. The most important role task is to support the group with innovative ideas on the way to the goal.

4. **Networker**

   Networkers establish contact with their environment. They recognise interfaces to other people and organisational components and are ready to undertake associated jobs. Their most important task is to communicate externally and to carry important information from the outside into the group.

5. **Team worker**

   Team workers are the unifying element in the group. They are concerned with creating harmony in the group and creating a pleasant working atmosphere. Their most important task is to constantly look at the cohesion of the group and take initiatives to improve it.

6. **Detailer/completer**

   This role works on and completes the group work in detail. Where other group members are already heading for new shores, this role has the need to round off the joint work. Their most important task is to find weak points in the details of the joint work and to eliminate them.

> The model of Gellert and Nowak is based on the more complex model of R. M. Belbin. For more information, see Belbin (2010).

Case Study

After John Smith had informed his sister about the topic of the workshop, the first thing she asked was about the group. John Smith was surprised at how interested his sister was in the details of the group. She asked about their relationships with each other. In particular, she asked about Mr. Wilson and his relationship with the group. John Smith told her that the relationship was strained and that there had already been frequent conflicts.

Amy Smith explained to him that, from her point of view, Mr. Wilson's attitude and behaviour in the workshop were crucial. Facilitation could only work if each group member was committed to working together as equals in the group. Amy suggested that she would first talk to Mr. Wilson in preparation for the workshop. In her view, a workshop would only make sense if Mr. Wilson was willing to engage in the group process. Otherwise, his behaviour towards the trainees would be more of a leadership issue for her brother as Mr. Wilson's superior than a working issue for the group.

Amy Smith spoke with Mr. Wilson the next day. The conversation lasted several hours and was very intense at times. At first, she noticed clear resistance on the part of Mr. Wilson. She addressed this and finally, they got to the core of the problem. Mr. Wilson had a deep-rooted fear of not being taken seriously or valued. To avoid the risk of being hurt in this way, he had given himself what he called a "thick skin".

3.3 · The Group

The moment this subject came up, something loosened in him. Only now could Amy Smith talk to him about the workshop. She came to the conclusion that Mr. Wilson's attitude now fitted the format of the facilitated workshop.

The less is known about the group at the beginning of the facilitation, the more important it is for the facilitator to get to know and classify the group at the beginning of the collaboration. We will address this in the following Chap. ▶ 4 when we examine the various steps of the facilitation process in more detail.

? Reflection Task
In the previous reflection task, you have already thought about the different groups to which you belong. Please look at them again (of course, you can also analyse other personal examples). What is your role in each group? Which role do you feel suits you best?

Summary in Key Terms
- Different people with different tasks are involved in the **facilitation process**: the client, the facilitator, and the group members.
  - The **client** decides to carry out the facilitation after determining,
  - that the **topic** is suitable for a facilitation process,
  - that facilitation as a measure fits in with the **corporate** and **working culture**,
  - what the **objectives** of the cooperation are and when they will be achieved,
  - what **room for manoeuvre** the facilitator and the group have.
- The **facilitator**
  - supports the client in finding clarity in the **specifications** mentioned above and in concretising the facilitation and group assignment,
  - develops the **dramaturgy** of the facilitated group work,
  - is responsible for **shaping the work process** of the group and supports them in a goal-oriented way in their **cooperation** (Freimuth, 2010; Graeßner, 2008).
  - combines three **roles**: the *problem solver*, the *conflict solver*, and the *reflector*.
  - can be based on the concept of **theme-centered interaction** (TCI) according to Ruth Cohn (1980), according to which the theme or task should be the focus of attention of all group members and should be worked on jointly by all.
    - In the model of theme-centered interaction, **three factors** are distinguished in an **environment (globe)**: I, the personality; We, the group; and It, the theme. These three factors meet in an environment that is defined by conditions such as time, place, and historical, social, and teleological circumstances.
    - Within the framework of TCI, the facilitator ensures that all three factors are **balanced** throughout the work process and that everything that takes place in the interaction fits the globe.

– From the assumptions of TCI, some **auxiliary rules** for the attitude and behaviour of the individual in the group interaction can be derived, as well as two **postulates** for the facilitated work process:
    1. Be your own chairperson.
    2. Disturbances take precedence.
 – should adopt a **personal attitude** that is oriented towards the human image of TCI and is fundamentally characterised by appreciation, respect, and approval.
- The **group**
    - consists of several members, each of whom is responsible for contributing their respective skills and information in order to work together to produce a **substantively viable outcome.**
    - The facilitator analyses the **structure** of the group to prepare for the facilitation process. In doing so, the facilitator focuses on the organisational embedding of the participants, the available resources, the interests, and the relationships between the group members (Freimuth, 2010; Gellert & Nowak, 2014).
    - can be analysed in terms of their **stage of group development** (Tuckman, 1965) as well as the different **roles within the group** (Gellert & Nowak, 2014).

References

Belbin, R. M. (2010). *Team roles at work* (2nd ed.). Butterworth-Heinemann.
Cohn, R. (1980). *Von der Psychoanalyse zur themenzentrierten Interaktion. Von der Behandlung einzelner zu einer Pädagogik [From psychoanalysis to theme-centred interaction. From the treatment of individuals to a pedagogy]* (4th ed.). Klett-Cotta.
Freimuth, J. (2010). *Moderation [Facilitation]*. Hogrefe.
Funcke, A., & Havenith, E. (2010). *Moderations-Tools. Anschauliche, aktivierende und klärende Methoden für die Moderations-Praxis [Facilitation tools. Illustrative, activating and clarifying methods for facilitation practice]*. ManagerSeminare.
Gellert, M., & Nowak, C. (2014). *Teamarbeit—Teamentwicklung—Teamberatung. Ein Praxisbuch für die Arbeit in und mit Teams [Teamwork—Team Development—Team Counselling. A practical book for working in and with teams]* (5th ed.). Christa Limmer.
Graeßner, G. (2008). *Moderation—das Lehrbuch [Facilitation – the textbook]*. Ziel.
Hartmann, M., Rieger, M., & Luoma, M. (1999). *Zielgerichtet moderieren. Ein Handbuch für Führungskräfte, Berater und Trainer [Facilitating purposefully. A handbook for managers, consultants and trainers]* (2nd ed.). Beltz.
Klebert, K., Schrader, E., & Straub, W. (2002). *Moderations-Methode. Das Standardwerk [Facilitation method. The standard work]*. Windmühle.
Langmaak, B. (1991). *Themenzentrierte Interaktion. Einführende Texte rund ums Dreieck [Theme-centred interaction. Introductory texts around the triangle]*. Psychologie Verlags Union.
Lubienetzki, U., & Schüler-Lubienetzki, H. (2016). *Sag mal: Wo geht's lang und wie kommen wir dahin? Moderation [Tell me: Which way is it and how do we get there? Facilitation] (Study letter of the Fresenius University of Applied Sciences online plus GmbH)*. Hochschule Fresenius online plus GmbH.

References

Lubienetzki, U., & Schüler-Lubienetzki, H. (2021). *Let's talk with each other! Psychology of successful conversation*. Springer.

Merriam-Webster. (n.d.). Postulate. In *Merriam-Webster.com dictionary*. Retrieved September 12, 2021, from https://www.merriam-webster.com/dictionary/postulate

Triandis, H. C. (1975). *Einstellungen und Einstellungsänderungen [Attitudes and attitude changes]*. Beltz.

Tuckman, B. W. (1965). Developmental sequence in small groups. *Psychological Bulletin, 63*(6), 384–399.

Watzlawick, P., Beavin, J. H., & Jackson, D. D. (1968). *Pragmatics of human communication. A study of interactional patterns, pathologies, and paradoxes*. Faber and Faber.

Always One Step at a Time

The Facilitation Process

Contents

4.1 The Contract – 33

4.2 The Preparation – 35

4.3 The Facilitated Group Work – 38
4.3.1 Start – 38
4.3.2 Content Work – 40
4.3.3 End – 43

4.4 Follow-Up – 43

References – 45

© Springer-Verlag GmbH Germany, part of Springer Nature 2022
U. Lubienetzki, H. Schüler-Lubienetzki, *Tell Me, Where Are We Going and How Do We Get There?*,
https://doi.org/10.1007/978-3-662-65588-7_4

Facilitation begins well before the actual group work and ends only after the group has dispersed. The facilitator is involved in all steps throughout. This does not necessarily have to be the case for the client and the group.

After reading this chapter in-depth, you will be able to …
- Identify the aspects that should be discussed by the client and the facilitator during the **clarification of the assignment.**
- **Prepare** for facilitated group work.
- Design the **introduction** to the facilitated group work as well as the **closing phase.**
- Explain the **components** of each facilitation and the facilitator's **role** during group work.
- **Follow up on** a facilitated group activity.

In ▶ Sect. 2.3 we had already presented an overview of the facilitation process. We remember (see ◘ Fig. 4.1).

Now, we will take a closer look at the individual steps. The decision to facilitate has been made and the task of facilitation needs to be defined.

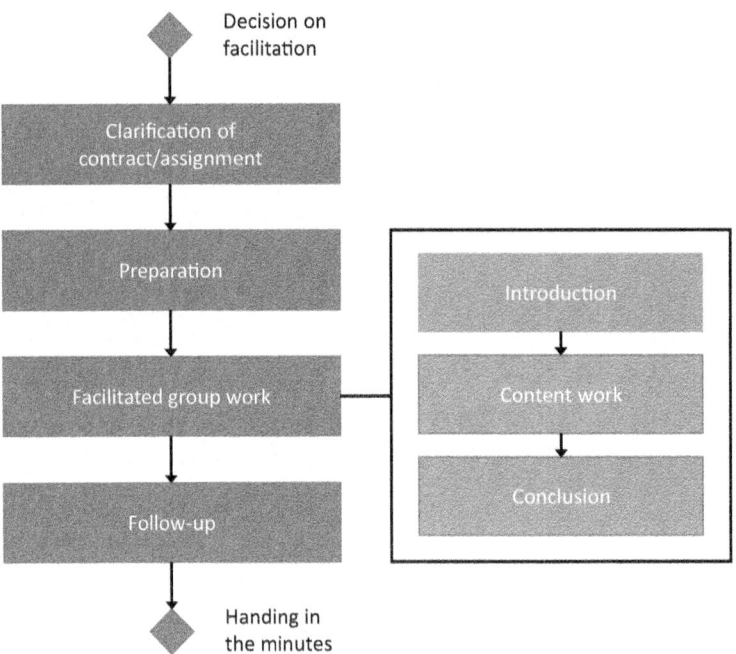

◘ Fig. 4.1 Facilitation process. The four steps of the facilitation process: clarification of the contract or assignment, preparation for the facilitation, the facilitation itself, and the follow-up to the facilitation. The process starts with the decision to facilitate and usually ends with the submission of the minutes (see Freimuth, 2010, p. 61)

4.1 The Contract

Before facilitation can start, the client should be clear about various points that are part of the assignments to the facilitator as well as to the group. These points should be specified in the contractual agreement with the facilitator at the latest. "**Contracting**", as Freimuth (2010, p. 49) calls this phase, includes not only the contract in the narrower sense but also various clarifications that the client and the facilitator should first bring about:

Regardless of whether the facilitation is carried out by a person inside or outside the organisation, the following points should be clarified. The individual points of the **assignment clarification** are based on Freimuth (2010) and Gellert and Nowak (2014):

1. **Objectives of the facilitation and mandate to the group**

    Objectives should be **SMART** and formulated according to **PPP**. This means that goals should be specific, measurable, accepted, realistic, and timed, and should be positively descriptive (i.e., formulate what is to be done, not what is not to be done), using the first-person point of view and present tense (Gellert & Nowak, 2014, p. 39). According to Freimuth, well-formulated and thought-out objectives determine the group's scope of action in the working phase and thereby allow the client and the facilitator to narrow down the variety of possible results. There is little room for manoeuvre if the group is purely brainstorming and collecting ideas. The scope is greater if an opinion is formed at the end or even scenarios and options are developed. Recommendations up to the point of a decision form a further enlargement. The most far-reaching result is that the group can make a concrete decision (Freimuth, 2010, p. 55).

2. **Issues, problems and attempted solutions**

    The topics to be dealt with should be narrowed down in terms of content. It should be clear to the participants what is ultimately to be worked on. Important framework conditions and limits should also be known in advance. Already known problem areas should be named and previous attempts at solutions should also be disclosed (Freimuth, 2010; Gellert & Nowak, 2014).

3. **Cultural conditions and composition of the group**

    An important question to be clarified in advance is whether facilitation is the appropriate means or method to address the issue or problem within the organisational culture. As discussed in ▶ Sect. 2.2, for example, strong hierarchical structures prevent the successful use of facilitation. The group itself should be analysed based on the points discussed in ▶ Sect. 3.3 "organisational embedding", "resources", "interests" and "relationship". In groups that have been working together for a longer period, questions can be asked about the phase of group development as well as about the roles in the group (Freimuth, 2010; Gellert & Nowak, 2014, as well as Tuckman, 1965).

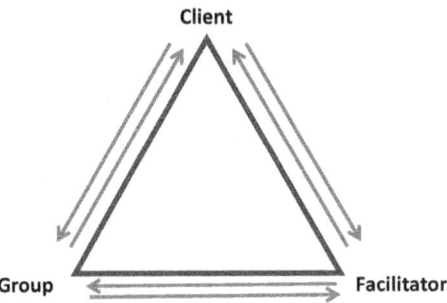

Fig. 4.2 Triangular contract within the facilitation process. The client, facilitator, and group each have a contract with each other. All participants should be aware of this triangular constellation and deal with each other as transparently as possible. Ideally, all contractual agreements are open and accessible to everyone. (Source: own representation based on Gellert & Nowak, 2014, p. 33)

4. **Requirements for the facilitator**
    In ▶ Sect. 3.2 the facilitator is described with their attitude as well as their roles and tasks. These factors should be taken into account when selecting a person as a facilitator (Freimuth, 2010; Funcke & Havenith, 2010; Graeßner, 2008).
5. **Methods, procedure, and technique**
    The methods, procedure, and technique are already part of the preparation of the facilitation and are contractually relevant insofar as the client is to make a contribution (e.g. provide rooms) (Freimuth, 2010).

The contract discussed so far is concluded between the client and the facilitator. In reality, two further contractual relationships arise, namely between the client and the group and between the facilitator and the group. This creates a "**triangular contract**" (Gellert & Nowak, 2014, p. 32) (see ▣ Fig. 4.2).

> **Definition**
>
> **Triangular contracts** involve three (or more) parties. (Gellert & Nowak, 2014, p. 32)

All participants should be aware of this constellation and ensure transparency. Ideally, the client discloses the contractual agreement to the group. If this is not done in advance, the facilitator informs the group about the contract at the beginning of the collaboration. The facilitator then agrees on the contract with the group. Discrepancies can arise here that need to be clarified with the client (Gellert & Nowak, 2014).

> **Case Study**
>
> It was important to John and Amy Smith that, despite (or perhaps because of!) their close family relationship, they should have a clear contractual arrangement regarding facilitation. Amy Smith, therefore, sat down with her brother and clarified her assignment with him. She already knew the company Construction Machines Smith Ltd. quite well. She had already spoken with Mr. Wilson and knew that the other group consisted of ten trainees. Both had already outlined the topics and the objective in the preliminary discussion. Now, it was just a matter of getting to the point. John Smith wanted the workshop to produce recommendations for cooperation in and with the group of trainees. He wanted to talk about the recommendations with Mr. Wilson afterward. Afterward, Mr. Wilson should decide as the person responsible for the trainees.
>
> Finally, they formulated the goal of the workshop as:
>
> "We (the group of trainees including Mr. Wilson) work out recommendations in a one-day workshop how the cooperation in our group should be designed in the future."

> **Important**
> In our view, it is worthwhile to formulate a contract or at least a written mandate even for internal facilitation. In human communication, many things can happen and might go wrong. If there is a written contract, it is much easier to establish a common understanding on the factual level.

4.2 The Preparation

The points clarified in the contract form the basis for preparing the facilitation. If individual aspects have not been dealt with in sufficient detail in the contractual clarification, the client should be asked as part of the preparation (Hartmann et al., 1999).

> **Important**
> In the context of facilitated team developments, we have had a good experience with asking the participants about their expectations in the run-up to the event. This allows the preparation to be tailored even more clearly to the group.

Planning the facilitation **procedure** is the focus of the preparation. The starting point is the goal and the task of the group work as well as the participants themselves. This determines how the introduction, the deepening, and the conclusion are designed in a way that is appropriate to the goal and the target group. Following Freimuth (2010); Hartmann et al. (1999) and Klebert et al. (2002), the following basic questions should be answered in the preparation:

1. **Launch**
   - How will I start and greet the group? How do we introduce ourselves?
   - How will I explain the agenda and objectives of the cooperation (clarified in the contract/order)?
   - How will I explain the specifics of facilitated collaboration to the participants? How will I explain the roles in our joint work?
   - How will I find out about expectations and the mood of the group?
   - What rules do we as a group agree on to guide us in our collaboration?
   - How will I present the process and our time frame?
   - How will I get the participants in the right mood for working together?
2. **Drilling deeper**
   - What agenda of collaboration will I offer to the group? Which working steps that I offer to the group will lead to the goal? What is the schedule of the collaboration?
   - Which (sub-)objectives and questions for processing the different working steps will I offer?
   - What procedures and methods will I offer to the group to work through the steps?
   - How will I visualise the facilitation procedures and methods?
   - How will we document the results in each individual working step?
3. **Close**
   - How will I design the action plan to implement the results of the work following the meeting?
   - What can I offer to the group to increase the likelihood that the actions will be realised?
   - How will I record the open topics of the group to be dealt with afterwards?
   - How will I align the goals and expectations with the results that have been developed?
   - How will I organise the group's feedback on the session and my facilitation?
   - How will I say goodbye to the group?

4.2 · The Preparation

> **Important**
> Similar to the planning of training events, it has proven useful in our experience to develop a plan according to the following pattern. The answers to the above questions are then incorporated into this plan.

Once the basic questions mentioned above and any specific questions that may have arisen have been answered and the plan for the workshop has been determined, the necessary **facilitation materials** should be prepared or made available as part of the preparation. If the facilitator does not provide the materials but someone else does, they should check them to avoid surprises in the session or workshop (Klebert et al., 2002).

> **Reflection Task**
> Please design your workshop. You are free to choose: Please take a workshop that will take place in the near future or one that has already taken place and that you would like to take a closer look at, or help Amy Smith with the one-day workshop with the trainees. Feel free to use the workshop template shown in ◘ Table 4.1 as a guide. First of all, please focus on the process, the goals and tasks, and the content. You will deal with the methodology and facilitation material later.

◘ Table 4.1 Workshop plan

Agenda item	Time	Goal/task	Content	Method/material
1	09:00–09:30	Welcome/entry	Welcome Targets Organisational matters	Flipchart presentation Pinboard
...	...	...	...	...

4.3 The Facilitated Group Work

The group work, workshop, or meeting has been planned and prepared. Now, it comes to implementation. According to the planning process, this is divided into introduction, content work, and conclusion. Let us now consider in ▶ Sects. 4.4.1, 4.4.3, and 4.4.5 some basic possibilities for structuring the various stages of the facilitation process—based on Freimuth (2010); Hartmann et al. (1999); Klebert et al. (2002); Funcke and Havenith (2010) and Graeßner (2008) as well as our own experience.

4.3.1 Start

One of the most challenging moments of facilitated group work is the beginning. This is true for the facilitator as well as for the group. The group is curious about what to expect and to what extent their expectations will be met. Although the facilitator will be well prepared, the transition from theory to practice is always fraught with uncertainty. As in any human communication process, the first step is to build up relationships between the facilitator and the group, as well as within the group (especially if the participants do not know each other well). Communication and work on the factual level can only be purposeful when the relationship level is clear and sustainable (see Lubienetzki & Schüler-Lubienetzki, 2021a, 2021b).

The beginning of the collaboration is more like a presentation. The facilitator welcomes the participants and introduces themselves. They introduce the group to organisational matters, facilitation, and the goals. The facilitator also allows the group to present themselves and their expectations. The duration of the initial phase depends on the extent to which the participants already know each other and on their overall attitude towards the event. Also, the initial phase should be balanced with the duration of the collaboration. For example, in an event that lasts only a few hours, it is hardly possible to include a longer initial sequence.

In a nutshell, when starting, you should succeed in …
1. establishing **contact** with the participants as well as among the participants,
2. creating a productive **working atmosphere** and, in particular, alleviating fears and reduce tensions,
3. opening up the participants for the topic and enabling them to **relate** the topic to themselves, as well as
4. **guiding** in all relevant matters.

> **Important**
> In the beginning, rambling explanations (e.g. about the facilitator) are rather counterproductive. You do not have to prove to the participants that you have mastered facilitation. The relationship level and the contact to the participants are more important. Appreciation, friendliness, and humour are good starting points for making positive contact with the participants.

4.3 · The Facilitated Group Work

Especially in the beginning, the own attitude as a facilitator should be checked again and again. The group works on the content and the facilitator supports the work process. The work content includes the goals of the event as well as the questions and work steps that are dealt with together. In this context, the facilitator should make suggestions to the group, which the group confirms, adapts, or rejects. Rules of cooperation should also be defined, which each participant should explicitly acknowledge.

> **Important**
> In our view, the following four rules of cooperation have proven to be the basis of cooperation in a workshop:
>
> 1. Commitment
> 2. Confidentiality
> 3. Confrontability
> 4. Self-responsibility
>
> This ensures that the participants are aware of their responsibility in working together, that safe space for cooperation is created and that disagreements and conflicts can be dealt with in a targeted manner. Depending on the situation and topic, these basic rules can and should of course be supplemented.

Let us take a look at two methods that we think are well suited for the introductory phase:

1. Sociometric positioning

    The participants position themselves in the room based on questions. They communicate with each other to determine their positioning in relation to each other and the room. Possibilities are, for example, that the participants form clusters (e.g. according to hobbies or first profession), align themselves in relation to a centre point (e.g. according to the degree of concern) or position themselves on an imaginary map (e.g. according to their place of birth). The advantage of sociometric positioning is that they take little time, give an overview and activate the participants as well as bring them into contact with each other.

Case Study

At the beginning of her facilitation, Amy Smith wants to activate the group and get it moving. Therefore, she chooses some sociometric positionings at the beginning. In this way she gets to know the group and the group also gets to know each other better. At the same time, everyone is moving and talking. As a simple introductory question, she asks about the place of birth. To do this, she draws up a virtual map of the country the workshop takes place in. She declares one side of the room as the country's eastern border, so the opposite side represents the western boundary, she also points out cities that lie in the northern side of the country and characterises the last side of the room as south by naming respective landscape features. The partici-

> pants should now position themselves on the imaginary map based on the question "Where were you born?"
>
> To get an idea of the mood of the group, she asks the question "On a scale of 1 to 10, how is your mood this morning? 10 stands for 'everything's great' and 1 for 'very bad'." The trainees and also Mr. Wilson line up accordingly, with one end of the line representing a value of 1 and the other end representing a value of 10 on the scale. While the participants sort themselves out, Ms. Smith addresses them, asks supplementary questions, and the participants among themselves also engage in lively conversation. They often smile and laugh.

2. **The sketched introduction**

   Two participants interview each other with four questions that can be related to the personal or professional background. For example (1) my professional task; (2) my most important expectation for the workshop; (3) my highlight of the last year; (4) something positively surprising about me. On a flipchart two big squares are drawn and quartered, so that each big square consists of four fields. The interviewee answers the questions, and the interviewer visualises the answers in the four fields of the first big square by drawing. Once the four questions have been answered, the roles are switched/reversed/swapped[?] and the other one fills in the four fields of the second big square. Afterwards, the interviewer introduces the interviewee in the plenary by the means of the four drawn answers, respectively.

> **Important**
> Often groups are reluctant to draw. When we ask the participants whether they can draw, we usually get the answer "no" or "very poorly". To open up the group, a change of perspective often helps. Ask participants to imagine a group of children and ask the question "What do you think a group of young children—for example, a kindergarten group—would answer to the question 'Can you draw?'" Usually the participants smile in response to the question, and after they have started drawing, they quickly overcome their hesitation.

> **Reflection Task**
> Please remember the workshops in which you have participated. How was the introduction methodically designed in each case? What did you like and what did you not like?

4.3.2 Content Work

Subsequent to the introduction, the actual goal-oriented content work follows. The division of work is such that the facilitator is responsible for the process and the group for the content work. All results coming out are the results of the group. In order for these results to be implemented, the group should be in agreement with everything that happens. The facilitator, therefore, offers their proposal for the course of the workshop or facilitated group work to the group and the group decides to what extent it will be implemented as suggested or with adjustments. In order to enable the group to make such a decision, the facilitator should explain each methodological step to the group and obtain their agreement. The facilitator can refer to this agreement in the further course in order to guide the group through passages in which they feel less certain The systematic introduction of the group to a methodological step should contain the following elements:

1. **Aim** of the step
2. **Justification** of the chosen methodological step
3. The organisational **procedure** of the step (group form, times, other working arrangements (e.g. room distribution, facilitation materials))
4. **Work task/question**

After the facilitator has explained these points to the group, questions of comprehension deriving from the group are clarified. Only when each participant has understood all of the points does the facilitator ask for the group's agreement to work on this step as discussed. Then the group work begins as agreed.

The results of each methodological step must be saved in order to make them available for subsequent steps. It is important that all results are available to all participants. If the group works in plenary, the facilitator ensures that the results are visible to all participants by means of suitable visualisation. If work takes place in small groups, the results should first be documented by the small groups themselves. The facilitator can support this by making suitable suggestions. The results of the small group work are then to be made available to the entire plenum. The facilitator is responsible for ensuring that the entire group is aware of all the results.

> **Case Study**
>
> Amy Smith offers the group to discuss in two small groups the question: "How can we improve our cooperation?" The objective of this step is to obtain a working basis based on which the group can subsequently plan concrete measures. In small groups, it is easier to ensure that everyone has their say and, in a shorter time, many answers can be worked out, which can then be processed in the plenary into an overall picture (e.g. with prioritisation).
>
> Amy Smith suggests 45 min as the time frame. The groups should write down the results of their work on cards, which should then be presented by the groups on a pinboard. The group agrees to the procedure and starts working in small groups.

Basic methods, tasks, and work forms run through every facilitation. The following points are **components of every facilitation**:

1. Group work forms and settings

    Group work forms and settings describe how cooperation is organised. The work form describes how the group is structured in the collaboration. The possibilities range from working together in the whole plenum to small groups with four to seven participants to groups of two or three. Particularly in the initial phase, it can be useful to design short sequences of individual work, so each member has the chance to find their individual access to the topic. The setting describes the spatial arrangement of the cooperation. The more open a topic, the more open the setting. In this context, **market-like settings** (i.e., "booths" on different topics are distributed throughout the room, participants can move freely around the room and freely decide which topics they want to deal with) create a very open atmosphere that promotes creativity (e.g., World Café, see ▶ Sect. 5.1.1), **circular settings** (e.g. chair circles) emphasise the equal aspect in the group and promote discussion, and **metric settings** (i.e. participants take their seats in a predetermined orientation, e.g. presentation, panel discussion) serve to convey information in a concentrated manner.

2. Questioning techniques

By asking questions, the facilitator helps the group to shed light on the working topic in a targeted manner, to find new perspectives and points of view, and to reflect on the status of work. To encourage conversation and discussion, questions should be open-ended. The questions should show genuine interest and arouse the group's curiosity. Finally, the questions should be understandable to all participants so that all can respond. Questions can be answered in an open discussion. The facilitator records the answers on a flipchart, for example. To visualise answers directly and make them more accessible for further processing, card or point queries can be used. In **card queries**, the answers are written on cards by the participants. They are then explained and put on a pinboard. In the **point enquiry,** the participants attach their answer(s) as a point or points to a predefined list or scale. This can be used, for example, to ask about priorities or rate the importance of a topic.

3. Visualisation

The visualisation of work content and results helps the group to understand and interpret them in the same way. It forces them to separate the important from the unimportant results and thus makes it easier for the participants to concentrate on the essentials. It also allows complex issues to be presented and communicated in a more comprehensible way. Finally, visualisation also serves as documentation, whereby the work status is visible and accessible to the entire group at all times. Various forms of visualisation can be used in the facilitation process. For example, the facilitator can provide **presentations** (e.g. with Microsoft PowerPoint) and posters (e.g. on a flipchart) prepared for group work. In group work, results can be recorded on the **flipchart**. Paper-covered **pinboards** are suitable for working with cards in different forms and at the same time directly noting down supplementary content (e.g. frames and headings for clusters).

4. Securing results

The results of the facilitated group work are to be documented and saved. The form in which the results are saved depends on the task and objective of the collaboration. Thus, one result can be an unprioritised or prioritised **list**. This list can contain topics or recommendations for further work. If this list is supplemented by responsible and supporting persons, by dates or periods as well as by criteria for their fulfilment, an **action catalogue** or plan is created. **Decisions** can also be made as a result. These should be documented in such a way that they can subsequently be made available to other participants and implemented. As points often arise in the discussion which, for various reasons, cannot be dealt with in the facilitated group session, a **topic memory** should be provided as one outcome. In the course of the cooperation, the open points are noted on a flipchart as a list and, at the end of the meeting, it is decided and recorded how these are to be dealt with in the follow-up.

❓ Reflection Task

Now, please take another look at your prepared workshop plan. The column method/material is still empty. Please consider which method is suitable for the respective work step. You can use the basic methods mentioned above as a first suggestion. Please research other methods and choose the one you think is most suitable. Finally, please add the material necessary for the implementation of the method.

4.3.3 End

The conclusion of the facilitated group work is initiated with the securing of results. For each participant, it becomes transparent what has emerged in terms of content—in relation to the previously defined goals and work tasks—in the collaboration. The list of results and/or the action plan are jointly adopted. The facilitator should also create a situation where the participants can appreciate or even celebrate the work they have completed together.

At the end of the group work, all participants should stand behind the results they have achieved. Finally, the participants are given the opportunity to comment on their expectations stated at the beginning and on the results achieved. If the expectations were not met, this should be documented in the topic memory. In addition, measures are to be defined for the next steps and for other open topics.

In addition to the content-related work, the acilitated work process is also to be reflected by the participants at the end of the facilitation process. Afterward, they share their feedback with the facilitator.

Finally, the facilitator says goodbye to the group as well as he gives the participants the opportunity to say goodbye to each other.

4.4 Follow-Up

The follow-up begins with the farewell of the group. The facilitator has the task of recording or documenting the results and, if applicable, the course of the group's work. Depending on the agreement with the group or the client, the facilitator provides only the final results or additionally all intermediate results and work statuses as photo documentation and/or as a transcript.

Summary in Key Terms

- After the decision to carry out facilitation, the contracting between the client and the facilitator takes place. The following points should be discussed:
    - The **scope** of the group as well as the **objectives** of the facilitation (formulated according to the concepts SMART and PPP).
    - Central **topics** and problems as well as previous **approaches to solving them.**
    - Cultural conditions and **composition** of the group.
    - **Requirements** for the facilitator.
    - Optionally methods, **procedure,** and technique.
- When **preparing** for facilitated group work, the facilitator prepares the required facilitation materials and plans...
    - the **introduction** to the cooperation (this means, among other things, the greeting; the gathering of goals and expectations; the explanation of the process and the game rules; the joint introduction),
    - the **procedure** during content-related work (the timeline; the processing of all sub-goals and questions; concrete methods, visualisation and securing of results),
    - the **conclusion** of the cooperation (preparation of an implementation plan; alignment of objectives, expectations, and results; feedback and farewell).
- The **introduction** to facilitated group work offers the group the opportunity to orient itself and activates the group members for the joint work.
    - Therefore, it is important to establish a **relationship** between the facilitator and the group, as well as among the group members, to create a productive working atmosphere and to get all participants in the mood for the topic.
    - Methods such as *sociometric positionings* or *the painted introduction* can be used to get started.
- During the **content-related work,** the facilitator actively contributes to shaping and supporting the work process; the group is responsible for the content and makes decisions.
    - The facilitator makes **suggestions** about the process, gives reasons, and explains them in detail. The group **decides** whether and with which adjustments the suggestions are implemented. The facilitator checks whether all participants have **understood** and **agreed** with the methodological processes and the results that emerge from them. In addition, they help to deal with or **eliminate disturbances** and makes sure that the group remains **able to work.**
    - **Components of each facilitation** are group work forms and settings, questioning techniques, visualisation, and securing of results.
- **Finally**, the results are secured appropriately, the joint work is reflected, feedback is given to each other, and farewells are said.
- After the group work, the facilitator does the follow-up of the collaboration in the form of a **protocol** or documentation and makes it available to the group or the client as agreed.

References

Freimuth, J. (2010). *Moderation [Facilitation]*. Hogrefe.

Funcke, A., & Havenith, E. (2010). *Moderations-Tools. Anschauliche, aktivierende und klärende Methoden für die Moderations-Praxis [Facilitation tools. Illustrative, activating and clarifying methods for facilitation practice]*. ManagerSeminare.

Gellert, M., & Nowak, C. (2014). *Teamarbeit—Teamentwicklung—Teamberatung. Ein Praxisbuch für die Arbeit in und mit Teams [Teamwork—Team Development—Team Counselling. A practical book for working in and with teams]* (5th ed.). Christa Limmer.

Graeßner, G. (2008). *Moderation—das Lehrbuch [Facilitation—The textbook]*. Ziel.

Hartmann, M., Rieger, M., & Luoma, M. (1999). *Zielgerichtet moderieren. Ein Handbuch für Führungskräfte, Berater und Trainer [Facilitating purposefully. A handbook for managers, consultants and trainers]* (2nd ed.). Beltz.

Klebert, K., Schrader, E., & Straub, W. (2002). *Moderations-Methode. Das Standardwerk [Facilitation Method. The standard work]*. Windmühle.

Lubienetzki, U., & Schüler-Lubienetzki, H. (2016). *Sag mal: Wo geht's lang und wie kommen wir dahin? Moderation [Tell me: Which way is it and how do we get there? Facilitation] (Study letter of the Fresenius University of Applied Sciences online plus GmbH)*. Hochschule Fresenius online plus GmbH.

Lubienetzki, U., & Schüler-Lubienetzki, H. (2021a). *How we talk to each other. The messages we send with our words and body language*. Springer.

Lubienetzki, U., & Schüler-Lubienetzki, H. (2021b). *Let's talk with each other! Psychology of successful conversation*. Springer.

Tuckman, B. W. (1965). Developmental sequence in small groups. *Psychological Bulletin, 63*(6), 384–399.

Special Settings and Challenges of Facilitation

Exceptional Groups and Recurring Pitfalls

Contents

5.1 **Large Group Procedures – 48**
5.1.1 World Café – 49
5.1.2 Open Space – 50

5.2 **Challenges and Pitfalls – 52**
5.2.1 Group Dynamic Effects at the Beginning of a Facilitated Session – 52
5.2.2 Planning Replaces Chance with Error – 53
5.2.3 Resistance in Groups – 53

References – 57

© Springer-Verlag GmbH Germany, part of Springer Nature 2022
U. Lubienetzki, H. Schüler-Lubienetzki, *Tell Me, Where Are We Going and How Do We Get There?*,
https://doi.org/10.1007/978-3-662-65588-7_5

Certain groups and situations sometimes pose special demands and challenges for the facilitator. For example, there are group sizes that, in addition to the work of the facilitator, can only be supported in a targeted manner by special settings and forms of cooperation. The following also applies to the field of facilitation: Anything can happen. On the one hand, this makes it so interesting and challenging, and on the other hand, it is, therefore, well worth being prepared for challenges that arise again and again.

After reading this chapter in-depth, you will be able to ...
- Identify and describe **facilitation procedures for large groups**.
  - Explain the large group methods *World Café* and *Open Space* and their backgrounds.
- Explain and appropriately address **challenges** in working with large groups.
  - Counteract negative **group dynamic effects** at the beginning of a facilitation process with the right introduction.
  - Explain why the facilitator needs to be flexible in **adapting** their **approach** to the group and not the other way round.
  - Identify **resistance** in a group as such and deal with it in a goal-oriented manner.

5.1 Large Group Procedures

So far in this book, we have dealt with groups of up to 20–25 participants. With more than 25 participants, we call it a **large group.** In principle, there is no upper limit to the size of large groups but there are practical limits when we consider that these groups need space, materials, and other logistical conditions to be able to work.

Due to the number of participants alone, large groups are no longer amenable to classic facilitation approaches and methods. Nevertheless, the need often arises to provide working formats for such large numbers of participants that go beyond pure frontal transfer of knowledge and information. In this sense, the public viewing of a football match is just as little a large group event as a conference with 1500 participants who listen to the presentations of three keynote speakers in 3 h and are allowed to ask questions for 5 min after each presentation (Dittrich-Brauner et al., 2013; Freimuth, 2010; Graeßner, 2008; Klebert et al., 2002).

We apply the following **criteria** when we speak of *facilitated large group procedures* (see Dittrich-Brauner et al., 2013):
1. More than 25 people are to work together in a targeted manner.
2. Cooperation should be given a defined framework.
3. A controlled and facilitated but open-ended process is run through together.
4. Working together to improve the system, processes, or relationships.
5. The self-responsibility and self-organisation ability of the participants is used and increased.

In the following, we will take a closer look at two large group processes: the World Café and Open Space.

5.1.1 World Café

The large group method **World Café** was developed in the mid-90s of the last century by Juanita Brown and David Isaacs (Brown & Isaacs, 2005). It is noteworthy that this method was not specifically developed for a large group but emerged spontaneously in the context of a classic workshop. Due to adverse weather conditions, an outdoor workshop could not take place as planned. Instead, a coffee house atmosphere was created in a room with various tables, flipchart paper as tablecloths, and coffee and croissants, which was spontaneously accepted by the participants. Only afterwards did Brown and Isaacs document their method and present it to the public. The name *World Café* says it all. A coffee house atmosphere is indeed created, which encourages the participants to exchange ideas in an informal conversational atmosphere, just like in a real coffee house. The process is designed to encourage large groups to exchange views creatively. It is less suitable for planning concrete measures and preparing or even making decisions in large groups. For this, other methods, such as action or planning groups, are needed to allow plans to emerge from the abundance of proposals or results (Dittrich-Brauner et al., 2013).

Adapted from Dittrich-Brauner et al. (2013), a World Café event runs according to the following **principles**:

1. **Carefully clarify the order.**
   As with classic facilitation formats, it is essential to clarify the goals and content of the event with the client in advance. If the goal is to discover new ideas or new approaches together and to exchange ideas creatively in a large group, the procedure is suitable for this. Action plans or decisions are not to be developed in the World Café.
2. **Take the term café or coffee house literally.**
   The World Café thrives on a pleasant and informal environment. It may smell of coffee, the tables may be decorated with fresh flowers and the entire room should remind of a coffee house.
3. **Ask relevant questions that pique curiosity.**
   The same or different questions can be discussed at the tables, which are occupied by four to five participants. It is important that the questions stimulate the participants to discuss.
4. **Encourage participants to get involved.**
   The small group atmosphere at the tables allows even the more reserved participants to contribute. Everyone is allowed to write down their thoughts—directly on the tablecloth.
5. **Provide a change of perspective.**
   The participants change tables at regular intervals. A "host" remains at each table, welcomes the new participants, and explains the state of the discussion.

After the change of tables, new questions can be introduced into the process or the change is structured in such a way that each table looks at a specific question, which is taken up and supplemented by the new 'guests'.

6. **Allow new insights to emerge for each participant and all together.**

    The informal atmosphere invites people to listen. The participants are encouraged not only to express their views on the topics but also to experience the views of many different people. This results in a valuable gain in knowledge for each participant and an overall benefit for the entire group.

7. **Share the results.**

    After several rounds and table changes, the findings should be brought together. The hosts of the tables summarise the results for the plenary. The labelled tablecloths form the basis for their presentation. The results of the tables should be documented and communicated across the board. For example, a marketplace situation can be created where the groups move between the tables and are introduced to the results by a participant at each table.

> **Case Study**
>
> The company Construction Machines Smith Ltd. has now existed for 11 years. John Smith had explained on different occasions and in different contexts to the employees and customers what kind of a Construction Machines Smith Ltd. is and which basic guidelines determine the work and cooperation. However, there was nothing of this kind formulated and accessible to everyone. Therefore, he made the decision to design a mission statement for Construction Machines Smith Ltd. Since all employees should identify with the mission statement, he also wanted to involve all employees in the development. He asked his sister for a suitable form of event, who spontaneously thought of the World Café.
>
> The central question should be: "What ideas do you have about the mission statement of Construction Machines Smith Ltd?"

? Reflection Task

Mr. Smith approaches you with the facilitation task of developing the mission statement of Construction Machines Smith Ltd. with the involvement of all employees. You suggest the large group method World Café to him. Please explain to Mr. Smith how you imagine the use of the World Café.

5.1.2 Open Space

The large group method **Open Space** goes back to Harrison Owen (2008), who used it for the first time in the mid-1980s. The idea for Open Space came from the observation that in the context of a classic conference, with plenary lectures and coffee breaks between the lecture blocks, the participants tended to be bored and often distracted during the lectures, and it was only during the coffee breaks that creative and inspiring conversations developed. The idea of Open Space is, therefore, to make the conversations and activities in the coffee breaks the actual focus of the conference.

In Open Space, a marketplace atmosphere is created in which all participants can turn to the stand or group that interests them most at a given moment. If a participant loses interest or notices that they are more interested in another group, they can change the group at any time. *Open Space* is to be understood literally. The participants are simply given a central theme or a question (e.g. "The future mission statement of Construction Machines Smith Ltd"). Then, passion and responsibility bring people together in the right constellation. This is achieved by not forcing anyone to participate. Open Space is voluntary and therefore only people meet who are interested in the topic and willing to take responsibility for it (Dittrich-Brauner et al., 2013).

Open Space starts in a circular setting (e.g. chairs in a circle, depending on the number of participants and the size of the room, several circles lying inside each other are also conceivable). In this way, the facilitator has the opportunity to address and reach all participants at the beginning. They explain the topic or the question and then leaves the field to the participants and opens the *free space*. There are no more guidelines. As a rule, rooms are available in which the participants can gather in the emerging groups, and facilitation materials (flipcharts, pinboards, facilitation kits, etc.) are provided. Who goes where and deals with which topic is absolutely up to all participants at all times. Initially, this approach often leads to uncertainty among the participants, as the entire further process is left up to them (Freimuth, 2010; Dittrich-Brauner et al., 2013).

Four guiding principles or guidelines define the Open Space process (Freimuth, 2010, p. 46; Dittrich-Brauner et al., 2013, p. 55):

1. "Whoever comes, it's the right people." or "Whoever comes, it's the right person."
2. "Whatever happens is the only thing that can happen."
3. "It starts when the time is right." or "It always starts at the right time."
4. "Gone is gone." or "When it's over, it's over."

The groups themselves are also responsible for visualisation and securing results. Sufficient flipcharts and pinboards should be available for this purpose (Dittrich-Brauner et al., 2013).

Large groups are a special situation and pose special challenges for the facilitator. Most of the time in facilitation we are dealing with much smaller group sizes. But even there, there are challenges and pitfalls that we have to handle. We will address these in the next section.

5.2 Challenges and Pitfalls

5.2.1 Group Dynamic Effects at the Beginning of a Facilitated Session

In ▶ Sect. 3.3 we looked at the group and its development. A group develops in four phases during the group process: orientation phase, position finding phase, organising phase, and working phase. The first two phases, in particular, are characterised by the fact that the members do not know each yet other or know each other only slightly, that the relationships between them are unresolved and that resistance and conflicts can arise in the process of clarification (Gellert & Nowak, 2014).

In the early phases of **group development**, i.e. at the beginning of facilitated group work, activities and methods should be used that take into account the possible insecurity of the participants. Especially at the beginning of facilitation, it is important to activate the participants without overwhelming them (Graeßner, 2008).

> **Important**
> We found the following example in a similar form in Graeßner (2008) and transferred it to the case study of Construction Machines Smith Ltd. and the facilitator Amy Smith.

Case Study

Amy Smith is a very experienced presenter. But even with her, not everything always goes smoothly. Just the other day, she underestimated the dynamics in a group during an initial sequence. She had assumed that there was a certain familiarity in the group because they had already been working together for some time. To activate the group, she had thought that all participants should take off their shoes, get onto their chairs in the circle of chairs and then arrange themselves according to their age without touching the floor. At her request, some participants looked surprised at first, others put a sheet of paper on the chair so as not to have to take off their shoes, and overall the exercise was characterised more by reserved distance than by active closeness.

After the workshop, she particularly evaluated this exercise and came to the conclusion that she had crossed and violated various boundaries of the participants at the beginning. Already taking off the shoes was a boundary for some participants which they didn't want to cross. The subsequent proximity to the other participants also caused significant discomfort. She concluded that this exercise was more suited to a group that was already very familiar with each other and where physical closeness was possible.

5.2.2 Planning Replaces Chance with Error

Good preparation is the most important basis of facilitation. In ▶ Sects. 4.1 and 4.2 we have dealt in detail with the questions that need to be clarified in the run-up to facilitation and everything that should be prepared. At the same time, the more meticulously a facilitation is prepared, the more likely it is that it will be necessary to deviate from the planned procedure.

The group determines what happens and what is worked out, not the facilitator. Therefore, the principle should be observed that the plan should be adapted to the group and its work and not vice versa. Forcing certain outcomes that would fit well with the plan will result in the facilitator losing the group and resistance is likely to arise (Graeßner, 2008).

> **Important**
> We also found this example in a similar form in Graeßner (2008) and applied it to the case study of Construction Machines Smith Ltd. and the facilitator Amy Smith.

Case Study

At the beginning of her work as a facilitator, Amy Smith had meticulously planned every step of the facilitation. In doing so she simply felt much more confident. As a result, she sometimes put her plan above the group, which led to the desired results but in the end, the group did not identify with the results.

In one of her first facilitations, she had been given a lot of cards after small group work. She had thought carefully about how she was going to sort the cards on the whiteboard. So she did this and the group watched. After sorting two-thirds of the cards, the result was already there, and she decided to put the remaining cards aside because of time constraints. The group was quiet at first. As time went on, resistance arose when the results were to be processed further. In the end, the participants were very reluctant to accept the results as theirs.

Already during the workshop, she realised her mistake: Her desire for her plan to work out was so great that she had worked out the results and not the group. Since then, she has been very careful to stay out of the content work.

5.2.3 Resistance in Groups

What applies to resistance in a conversation between two people (see Lubienetzki & Schüler-Lubienetzki, 2021) also applies to resistance in groups. We define the term **resistance** as follows:

> **Definition**
>
> **Resistance** is anything that prevents us from achieving our goals when communicating with others.

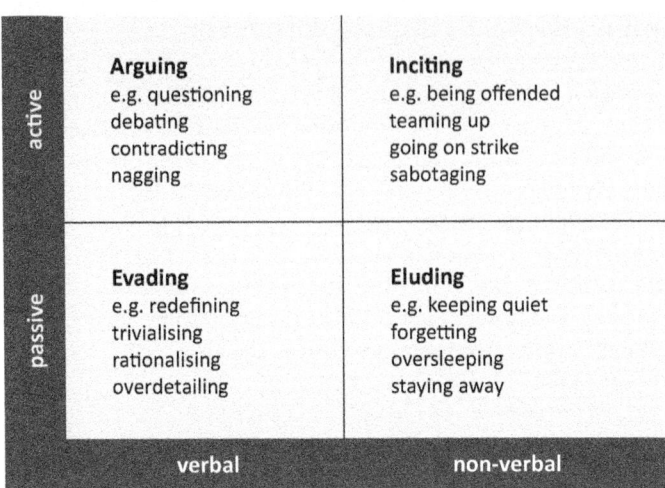

Fig. 5.1 Manifestations of resistance. Resistance can be active or passive and expressed verbally or non-verbally. The manifestations are manifold. (Source: Gührs & Nowak, 2014, p. 278)

The matrix in Fig. 5.1 shows how resistance can be expressed.

In a conversation between two people, resistance means that one person stands in the way of the other person achieving their goal. In facilitated group work, the resistance of a single participant can lead to other participants also resisting. For example, a group member can show resistance by agitating and thereby deliberately encourage other participants to resist as well (Gührs & Nowak, 2014).

If we as facilitators sense resistance in the group, we need to react appropriately. To start with, we need to find out what the resistance is directed against. According to Gührs and Nowak, resistance in working with groups can be directed against "the topic", "the process", "the framework conditions" or "the leader"/the facilitator (Gührs & Nowak, 2014, p. 281). Facilitators might tend to hastily direct the resistance towards themselves. If the resistance is directed against something else, this self-reference would lead to inappropriate reactions, which in turn could trigger actual resistance against oneself (Gührs & Nowak, 2014).

A goal-oriented **intervention**, i.e. a targeted measure or reaction by which we want to achieve a certain effect with our interlocutor, can only be successful if we know the motif that lies behind the resistance sufficiently well (Gührs & Nowak, 2014).

> **Definition**
>
> An **intervention** is "generally, any action intended to interfere with and stop or modify a process (…)" (American Psychological Association, n.d.).

The second relevant dimension is the impact of resistance. As the negative impact of resistance on achieving our personal goal increases, our reaction changes

5.2 · Challenges and Pitfalls

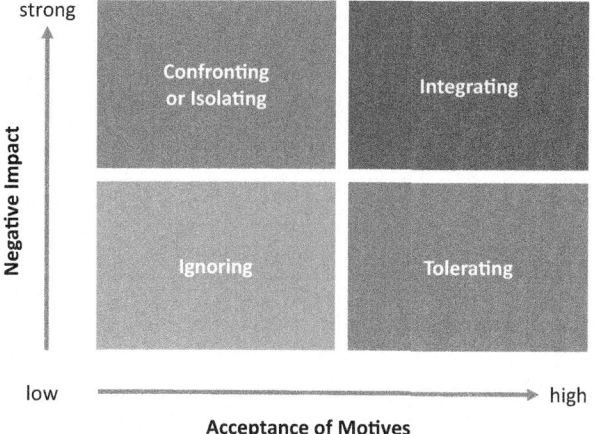

Fig. 5.2 Intervention strategies for resistance. Depending on the negative impact of the resistance and the own acceptance of the motives behind the resistance, different intervention strategies result. If the negative impact is low, the best strategy is often to do nothing and ignore the resistance. (Source: Gührs & Nowak, 2014, p. 282)

likewise. In one extreme our interlocutor offers resistance, but this is almost meaningless for achieving our goal. Consequently, we do not necessarily have to react to the resistance (Gührs & Nowak, 2014).

If we span a matrix between our acceptance of the motives of resistance and its negative impact, the intervention strategies in ◘ Fig. 5.2 (Gührs & Nowak, 2014) emerge.

Resistance is a central issue if we want to interact with people in a purposeful way. The pitfall is not resistance as such but handling it inappropriately.

Following Gührs and Nowak (2014), the following **intervention strategies** are possible in conversations—and also in facilitation processes:
1. **Ignore**: We perceive resistance but do not react to a participant's resistance.
2. **Tolerate**: Similar to isolating, we perceive the resistance but, in this case, we react to it. Our reaction should especially signal understanding but without giving it too much space.
3. **Confront**: Resistance is more massive and disruptive to the flow of the conversation. We confront a participant with their behaviour with the aim of changing it. In a group situation, it is often useful to confront a participant alone, i.e. to isolate them beforehand (e.g. to address them in a coffee break separated from the other participants).
4. **Integrate**: In this case also, the resistance is so disruptive that the achievement of the goal is jeopardised. Such a disturbance needs to be dealt with. Since we understand the motive, we signal our understanding and offer to integrate the subject of resistance into the group's work.

> **Important**
> In the book "Let's Talk with Each Other" (Lubienetzki & Schüler-Lubienetzki, 2021, Chap. 4), we deal with the topic of resistance in detail. There you will find examples and further information on the individual intervention strategies.

> **Reflection Task**
> Resistance is something very human. Surely, you have already resisted yourself or experienced other people in resistance. What did you or the other person put up resistance against? What behaviour did you show or experience? What was the effect of the resistance behaviour? What was your motive for resisting at the time, or what motive did you suspect the others had? How did the person affected by the resistance react at the time? How would you have reacted to the resistance with your current knowledge in the situation at that time?

> **Summary in Key Terms**
> - We speak of **large groups** when there are 26 or more participants.
> - Special **large group methods** such as the *World Café* or *Open Space* exist for such group sizes. Both methods are suitable for activating the creative potential of large groups and, in particular, for developing diverse ideas on a given topic (Dittrich-Brauner et al., 2013).
>   - The **World Café** allows for a creative exchange of opinions in a coffee house atmosphere.
>   - The **Open Space** method creates a marketplace atmosphere where participants can move freely between groups and engage in conversations according to their interests.
> - Working in or with large groups poses **special challenges** for the facilitator.
>   - Therefore, it is important to consider **group dynamics** and thereby the **developmental phases** of groups when choosing working methods (Gellert & Nowak, 2014).
>   - Despite thorough preparation for the facilitation, the facilitator should always be prepared to **deviate** from their **plan** if necessary and to flexibly **adapt** their approach to the group and its work content (Graeßner, 2008).
>   - Finally, there may occur **resistance** in the cooperation with the group, which must be countered in a targeted and appropriate manner (Gührs & Nowak, 2014).
>   - The **intervention strategy** is selected depending on the **motive** of the resistance and the **negative impact** on the achievement of the cooperation goal.

References

American Psychological Association. (n.d.). Intervention. In *APA dictionary of psychology*. Retrieved September 14, 2021, from https://dictionary.apa.org/intervention

Brown, J., & Isaacs, D. (2005). *The World Café. Shaping our futures through conversations that matter*. Berrett-Koehler.

Dittrich-Brauner, K., Dittmann, E., List, V., & Windisch, C. (2013). *Interaktive Großgruppen. Change-Prozesse in Organisationen gestalten [Interactive large groups. Designing change processes in organisations]* (2nd ed.). Springer.

Freimuth, J. (2010). *Moderation [Facilitation]*. Hogrefe.

Gellert, M., & Nowak, C. (2014). *Teamarbeit—Teamentwicklung—Teamberatung. Ein Praxisbuch für die Arbeit in und mit Teams [Teamwork—Team Development—Team Counselling. A practical book for working in and with teams]* (5th ed.). Christa Limmer.

Graeßner, G. (2008). *Moderation—das Lehrbuch [Facilitation—the textbook]*. Ziel.

Gührs, M., & Nowak, C. (2014). *Das konstruktive Gespräch. Ein Leitfaden für Beratung, Unterricht und Mitarbeiterführung mit Konzepten der Transaktionsanalyse [The Constructive Conversation. A guide for counselling, teaching and staff management with concepts from transactional analysis]* (7th ed.). Christa Limmer.

Klebert, K., Schrader, E., & Straub, W. (2002). *Moderations-Methode. Das Standardwerk [Facilitation method. The standard work]*. Windmühle.

Lubienetzki, U., & Schüler-Lubienetzki, H. (2016). *Sag mal: Wo geht's lang und wie kommen wir dahin? Moderation [Tell me: Which way is it and how do we get there? Facilitation] (Study letter of the Fresenius University of Applied Sciences online plus GmbH)*. Hochschule Fresenius online plus GmbH.

Lubienetzki, U., & Schüler-Lubienetzki, H. (2021). *Let's talk with each other! Psychology of successful conversation*. Springer.

Owen, H. (2008). *Open space technology. A user's guide* (3rd ed.). Berret-Koehler.

Overall Summary in Key Terms

Contents

References – 63

© Springer-Verlag GmbH Germany, part of Springer Nature 2022
U. Lubienetzki, H. Schüler-Lubienetzki, *Tell Me, Where Are We Going and How Do We Get There?*,
https://doi.org/10.1007/978-3-662-65588-7_6

- We encounter the term facilitation in various contexts in everyday life. The definitions of facilitation are just as diverse.
- We define **facilitation** as the goal-oriented support of the communication of people in groups.
  - In this context, the facilitator can also be understood as a **catalyst**.
- Facilitation aims to support the groups' decision-making and their communication, to use the existing potentials, and to promote motivation and satisfaction.
  - The **success** of facilitation is **influenced** by the working conditions and environment and communication breakdowns during the collaboration as well as by the competencies of the facilitator and the group members.
  - In the case of problems or alternatives with a high degree of complexity and/or involvement of the group members' interests, **management** is an **alternative** to facilitation.
  - For the most part, the various communication challenges in groups can be better managed with facilitation. However, this can bring other problems with it. **Problems** that can occur in connection with facilitation are suboptimal use of information, group think, entrapment, or decision autism (Freimuth, 2010).
- In this book, we understand facilitation as a **process** with three parties involved and four steps:
  1. **Clarification of contract** or **assignment** between client and facilitator
  2. **Preparation** by the facilitator
  3. Facilitated **group work** with the facilitator and the group
  4. **Follow-up** by the facilitator
- Before a **client** decides to conduct facilitation and selects a facilitator, they should consider ... (Freimuth, 2010; Hartmann et al., 1999).
  - whether the topic/problem in question is *suitable* for facilitation,
  - whether facilitation as a procedure fits in with the *corporate* and *working culture*,
  - which *goals* the facilitation should pursue,
  - what *room for manoeuvre* the group will have,
  - what *requirements* the facilitator must meet and what *criteria* are used to select them.
- When the client and the facilitator **conclude the contract** (so-called contracting), they clarify...
  - the *objectives* of the facilitation, in the best case, formulated according to the SMART and PPP concepts,
  - the *mission* to the group and its *scope of action*,
  - the central *topics/questions/problems* as well as previous *approaches to solving them*,
  - the cultural *conditions* and the *composition* of the group,
  - the *requirements* the facilitator has to meet,
  - if desired, the planned *approach* with methods and technology as well as *framework conditions*.

Chapter 6 · Overall Summary in Key Terms

- In theory, there is only a written contract between the client and the facilitator but in reality, there are also **contractual relationships** between the client and the group and between the group and the facilitator.
- A contract to which three or more persons are parties is called a **triangular contract.**
- In **preparing** for facilitated group work, the facilitator prepares the facilitation materials needed and plans …
  - the **introduction** to the collaboration (i.e., the welcome; the gathering of goals and expectations; the explanation of the process and the game rules; the joint introduction),
  - the **procedure** during the content-related work (i.e., the time planning; the processing of all sub-goals and questions; concrete methods, visualisation and securing of results),
  - the **conclusion** of the collaboration (i.e., the creation of an implementation plan; alignment of goals, expectations, and results; feedback and farewell).
- In preparation, the facilitator analyses the **group structure**, if possible, taking into account the organisational embedding of the participants and their resources, as well as the different interests and relationships among them (Freimuth, 2010; Gellert & Nowak, 2014).
- In principle and with all preparation, the facilitator must be prepared for the fact that not everything will go according to their plan. They must be **flexible** and **adapt** their approach to the circumstances if the situation, the group or the content developed demands it.
- At the **beginning of** the facilitated group work, contact is established with and among each other, a productive working atmosphere is created, and the group is introduced to the topic. This usually involves a round of introductions, during which the participants' expectations of the facilitated work process are also discussed and the organisational framework is clarified.
  - In the beginning, it is important to establish the **relationship** between the group and the facilitator as well as the relationship between the group members.
  - **Group dynamic effects** at the beginning of facilitation can pose a challenge to the facilitator, so the introduction should be designed with care.
  - *Sociometric positionings* or *the painted introduction* can be used as exemplary methods for an introduction.
- At the **end of** the facilitated group work, the facilitator checks that all participants are aware of and agree with all the results developed. Furthermore, the expectations expressed at the beginning of the session are compared with the elaborated results, and deviations are discussed. Finally, the joint work can be reflected and feedback given before saying goodbye to each other.
- The **follow-up** of the facilitated group work starts after the farewell. The facilitator prepares a protocol containing all the results achieved and, if necessary, information on the course of the group work. Depending on the agreement

with the group or the client, the protocol, including intermediate and final results, is made available to all.
- The **task** of the facilitator during the actual group work is to **support the working process** of the group as a **neutral** authority.
    - There is a clear **division of work**: the facilitator stays completely out of the content-related work and refrains from any form of evaluation or assessment of the work results.
    - The facilitator offers the group goal-oriented **methods**. They make **suggestions**, gives reasons for them, and explains the individual steps in detail. The group then decides whether and with which adjustments a proposal is to be implemented. In doing so, the facilitator obtains the consent of all participants and makes sure that all uncertainties are clarified.
    - In case of disturbances or impairments of the group's ability to work, the facilitator offers **assistance** by reflecting on what they experience in the group. This transparency, coupled with goal-oriented methods for **dealing with disturbances**, puts the group back on the path of constructive and successful cooperation.
    - Furthermore, the facilitator is responsible for **visualising** and **securing** the **results of** the group work. For this purpose, they provide facilitation materials, such as presentations, flipcharts, or pinboards, and ensures comprehensible and complete documentation of the developed contents.
- The facilitator can, in short, take on three roles: problem-solver, conflict-solver, and reflector.
- The facilitator can be guided by the approach of **theme-centered interaction** (TCI) according to Ruth Cohn (1980).
    - According to TCI, **three factors** interact in an **environment** or context (the Globe). These three factors are (1) I/personality, (2) we/group, and (3) it/the subject.
    - The facilitator makes sure that all three factors are **balanced** throughout the work process, with emphasis at times. Everything that takes place in the interaction must fit the globe.
    - The main **postulates** of theme-centered interaction are "Be your own chairperson." and "Disturbances take precedence."
    - In addition, TCI establishes various **auxiliary rules** which can guide the attitude and behaviour of the group members.
- The **basic attitude** of the facilitator should be characterised by appreciative interaction, helping and supportive behaviour, absolute neutrality as well as curiosity, and genuine interest in the people and their topics.
- The **group** is responsible for the **content** of the **work** and its **results**. Therefore, each group member should bring all available relevant information and their competencies into the work process.
    - The group can be classified into different **stages of group development** during the facilitated work process (Tuckman, 1965).
    - Multiple **roles within a group** can be differentiated (Gellert & Nowak, 2014).

- It is possible that the facilitator may perceive **resistance** in the group.
  - Resistance has different **manifestations**: it can be active and passive, verbal and non-verbal.
  - In facilitated group work, the resistance of one person can cause others to resist as well.
  - What is decisive is not the resistance itself but how the facilitator deals with it.
    - **Intervention** in case of resistance can only lead to the goal if the **motive** of the resistance is known. The facilitator must, therefore, find out what the resistance refers to and should not hastily relate it to themselves.
    - The **negative effect** of resistance on the achievement of goals or facilitated group work is crucial for the need for intervention.
    - Depending on the motive and the negative impact, the **intervention strategies** ignorance, tolerance, confrontation, and integration may be applied.
- If there are more than 25 participants, it is a **large group**. These require special procedures to support cooperation. Two **large group procedures** that have proven their worth are *World Café* and *Open Space*.
  - *World Café* allows for a creative exchange of opinions in small groups in a coffee house atmosphere, with tablecloths serving to secure the results.
  - In the *Open Space* process, participants move freely between groups in a marketplace atmosphere and can engage in various discussions on a guiding question or an overarching theme, depending on their interests.

References

Cohn, R. (1980). *Von der Psychoanalyse zur themenzentrierten Interaktion. Von der Behandlung einzelner zu einer Pädagogik [From psychoanalysis to theme-centred interaction. From the treatment of individuals to a pedagogy]* (4th ed.). Klett-Cotta.

Freimuth, J. (2010). *Moderation [Facilitation]*. Hogrefe.

Gellert, M., & Nowak, C. (2014). *Teamarbeit—Teamentwicklung—Teamberatung. Ein Praxisbuch für die Arbeit in und mit Teams [Teamwork—Team Development—Team Counselling. A practical book for working in and with teams]* (5th ed.). Christa Limmer.

Hartmann, M., Rieger, M., & Luoma, M. (1999). *Zielgerichtet moderieren. Ein Handbuch für Führungskräfte, Berater und Trainer [Facilitating purposefully. A handbook for managers, consultants and trainers]* (2nd ed.). Beltz.

Lubienetzki, U., & Schüler-Lubienetzki, H. (2016). *Sag mal: Wo geht's lang und wie kommen wir dahin? Moderation [Tell me: Which way is it and how do we get there? Facilitation] (Study letter of the Fresenius University of Applied Sciences online plus GmbH)*. Hochschule Fresenius online plus GmbH.

Tuckman, B. W. (1965). Developmental sequence in small groups. *Psychological Bulletin, 63*(6), 384–399.

Supplementary Information

Glossary - 66

Index - 69

© Springer-Verlag GmbH Germany, part of Springer Nature 2022
U. Lubienetzki, H. Schüler-Lubienetzki, *Tell Me, Where Are We Going and How Do We Get There?*,
https://doi.org/10.1007/978-3-662-65588-7

Glossary

Attitude (synonymous with personal attitude) An attitude is "an idea charged with emotion which predisposes a class of actions to a particular class of social situations." (Triandis 1975, p. 4)

Catalyst A catalyst is "a substance that causes or speeds a chemical reaction without itself being changed." (Cambridge University Press, n.d., see Sect. 2.4)

Contracting Contracting refers to the phase of clarifying the assignment and contract in the facilitation process, in which the client and the facilitator are involved and discuss various aspects relevant to the assignment (Freimuth, 2010).

Decision autism The term decision autism describes a group's pursuit of self-affirmation while closing their eyes to other options (Freimuth, 2010).

Entrapment Entrapment refers to a phenomenon occurring in later stages of group work in which the group is caught up in its previous results and persistently sticks to the chosen path despite disadvantages without admitting mistakes (Freimuth, 2010).

Facilitation Facilitation purposefully supports the communication of people in groups (own definition based on Freimuth, 2010; Klebert et al., 2002; Graeßner, 2008, and Hartmann et al., 1999).

Form of group work The form of group work describes how a group is structured in its cooperation; the possibilities range from cooperation in the whole plenum to small groups with four to seven participants to groups of two or three.

Group Think Group Think is an expression for a group's excessive striving for consensus with the effect that it overestimates itself and reacts narrow-mindedly and with social pressure to dissenting opinions (Freimuth, 2010).

Intervention An intervention is "generally, any action intended to interfere with and stop or modify a process" (American Psychological Association, n.d.).

Large group In facilitation, a large group is a group with more than 25 participants.

Management Management can generally be understood "as the process of planning, organizing, directing, and controlling the activities of employees in combination with other resources to accomplish organizational objectives." (Black & Bright, 2019)

Glossary

Open Space Open Space refers to a facilitated large group process in which participants move freely between groups in a marketplace atmosphere and can engage in various conversations on an overarching topic depending on their interests (Freimuth, 2010; Dittrich-Brauner et al., 2013).

Postulate A postulate is "a hypothesis advanced as an essential presupposition, condition, or premise of a train of reasoning" (Merriam-Webster, n.d., see Sect. 3.4).

Resistance Resistance is anything that prevents us from achieving our goals when communicating with others.

Setting The setting of a facilitated group work consists of the spatial arrangement of the collaboration, which can be, for example, market-shaped, circular, or metric.

Triangular contract Triangular contracts involve three (or more) parties (Gellert & Nowak, 2014).

World Café World Café refers to a facilitated large group process that allows for a creative exchange of opinions in small groups in a coffeehouse atmosphere, with participants moving between tables (Dittrich-Brauner et al., 2013).

Index

A

Attitude 21
Attitude, personal 11, 17, 18, 21, 22, 28
Auxiliary rule 20, 21, 28, 62
Axiom 7, 19

C

Catalyst 7, 13, 60
Challenge 3, 7–9, 48–56, 60, 61
Client 16
Coffee house 49
Cohn, Ruth 16, 18–21, 27, 62
Conflict 6–8, 10, 11, 13, 22, 24, 26, 39, 52
Content 40–43
Contract 12, 13, 18, 32–36, 60, 61
Contracting 16–18, 33, 44, 60

D

Decision autism 11
Disturbances 11

E

End 43
Entrapment 11

F

Facilitation 7
Facilitator 18–23
Factor 2, 11, 16, 18, 19, 27, 62

G

Group 2, 6–13, 16–28, 32–36, 38–44, 48–56, 60–63
– development 24, 52
– think 11

I

Image of man 21, 28
Interaction
– topic-centered 18
Intervention 54

L

Large group 48–50, 56, 63
Leadership 9
Line-up 40

M

Management 10, 11, 13, 60
Marketplace 51
Material 37, 41, 43, 44, 48, 51, 61, 62

O

Objectives 10
Open space 50
Ordering 2, 6, 9, 10, 16–19, 21, 28, 36, 40, 41

P

Personal attitude 21
Planning 53
Postulates 19
Presentation 37, 38, 42, 48, 50, 62
Problem 6, 7, 9, 11, 13, 16, 17, 21, 22, 26, 27, 44, 60, 62
Procedure 2, 36, 41, 44, 48–51, 53, 60, 61, 63
Process 2, 3, 6–8, 11–13, 16–28, 32, 35–44, 48–52, 54, 55, 60–63

Q

Questioning technique 42

R

Reflection 6, 10, 12, 19, 21, 23, 24, 27, 37, 40, 43, 50, 56
Relationship 2, 11, 21, 23, 24, 26, 35, 38, 44, 61
Resistance 53
Result 2, 7–11, 18, 19, 22, 23, 25, 36, 40–44, 49–51, 53, 61–63
Role components 22
Roles 24

S

Securing results 42
Selection 10, 17
Setting 41, 42, 44, 48, 49, 51–53, 55, 56
Sketched introduction 40
Sociometric positioning 39

Start 2, 33, 36, 54
Structure 6, 11, 16, 22, 23, 25, 28, 61
Subject 9, 27, 55, 62
Surroundings 25

T

Theme-centered interaction (TCI) 16, 18–21, 27, 62
Triangular contract 34

V

Visualisation 42

W

World Café 42, 48–50

The manufacturer's authorised representative in the EU is Springer Nature Customer Service Centre GmbH, Europaplatz 3, 69115 Heidelberg, Germany. If you have any concerns regarding our products, please contact ProductSafety@springernature.com

Printed and bound by CPI Group (UK) Ltd, Croydon, CR0 4YY

23/03/2026

02076369-0001